StyleCity
ATHENS

StyleCity
ATHENS

With over 300 colour photographs and 5 maps

ΚΟΥΡΕΙΟΝ

Contents

Street Wise

Style Traveller

Series concept and editor: Lucas Dietrich
Jacket and book design: Grade Design Consultants
Original design and map concept: The Senate
Maps: Peter Bull

Research and photographs by Julia Klimi
Texts by Ioanna Kopsiafti

First published in the United Kingdom in 2006 by
Thames & Hudson Ltd, 181A High Holborn,
London WC1V 7QX

www.thamesandhudson.com

British Library Cataloguing-in-Publication Data
A catalogue record for this book is available from the
British Library

ISBN-13: 978-0-500-21019-2
ISBN-10: 0-500-21019-5

Printed in China by C & C Offset Printing Co Ltd

How to Use This Guide

The book features two principal sections: **Street Wise** and **Style Traveller**.

Street Wise, which is arranged by neighbourhood, features areas that can be covered in a day (and night) on foot and includes a variety of locations – cafés, shops, restaurants, museums, performance spaces, bars – that capture local flavour or are lesser-known destinations.

The establishments in the **Style Traveller** section represent the city's best and most characteristic locations – 'worth a detour' – and feature hotels (**sleep**), restaurants (**eat**), cafés and bars (**drink**), boutiques and shops (**shop**) and getaways (**retreat**).

Each location is shown as a circled number on the relevant neighbourhood map, which is intended to provide a rough idea of location and proximity to major sights and landmarks rather than precise position. Locations in each neighbourhood are presented sequentially by map number. Each entry in the **Style Traveller** has two numbers: the top one refers to the page number of the neighbourhood map on which it appears; the second number is its location.

For example, the visitor might begin by selecting a hotel from the **Style Traveller** section. Upon arrival, **Street Wise** might lead him to the best joint for coffee before guiding him to a house-museum nearby. After lunch he might go to find a special jewelry store listed in the **shop** section. For a memorable dining experience, he might consult his neighbourhood section to find the nearest restaurant crossreferenced to **eat** in **Style Traveller**.

Street addresses are given in each entry, and complete information – including email and web addresses – is listed in the alphabetical **contact** section. Travel and contact details for the destinations in **retreat** are given at the end of **contact**.

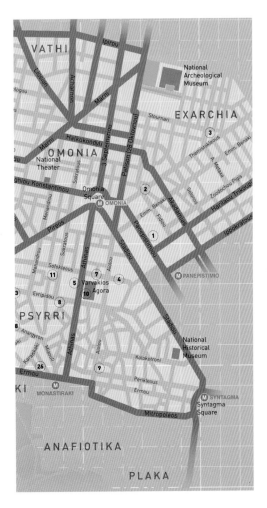

Legend

(**2**)	Location
▮	Museums, sights
▮	Gardens, squares
(**M**)	Metro stops
▦	Streets

ATHENS

Described by Lord Byron as the 'place I preferred on the whole to any I have seen', Athens blurs the line between myth and reality, history and legend, and inspires the imagination as no other city in the world. Named for the goddess of wisdom, Athens' past is ever-present in the majestic vision of the Parthenon hovering above the city. The sacred buildings of the Acropolis symbolize Greece's Golden Age, an extraordinary flourishing of art, philosophy, and government that 2,500 years later continues to enlighten humanity. For first-time visitors these ancient sites are a must, yet few people know the beauty of Athens' modern face. This is a city of opposites, of antiquity and modernity, and calm amidst chaos. Ask any Athenian what he is doing and the answer is likely to be *treho* ('running'); ask him out for coffee or an impromptu *ouzo* and suddenly he has all the time in the world. There is much more to this city than ancient temples, and each year visitors outnumbering the country's entire population converge upon it, each with his own expectation of the city.

Goethe claimed that 'of all peoples, Greeks have dreamt the dream of life best'. Today modern-day bon viveurs pursue the good life in Athens with enthusiasm, from simple pleasures to more cosmopolitan pursuits. After a cold winter Athenians like to spend as much time as possible outdoors, in streetside cafés, seaside clubs, or restaurant-bars for dining al fresco and dancing under the stars. Year-round sunshine has led to a thriving outdoor culture, in which lingering for hours over coffee is not so much a luxury as a way of life. The city also boasts an indefatigable nightlife. Athenians rarely dine before 10:00 p.m., venturing out to clubs only after midnight. With venues that feature everything from *rembetika* to *bouzoukia*, plus a calendar full of religious holidays and public festivals, 'everything in moderation' is a phrase that does not apply after dark in Athens. For the gastronome, dining options range from traditional tavernas to the new wave of modern restaurants that offer contemporary interpretations of classic Greek dishes alongside new trends in Mediterranean cuisine. The past 10 to 20 years have also seen the establishment of numerous state-of-the-art wineries, resulting in the development of a new range of world-class wines.

Athens' staging of the 2004 Summer Olympics brought a much-needed upgrade to the city's infrastructure, including an ultra-modern airport, traffic-alleviating ring roads, and an immaculate new Metro, together with a museum that preserves ancient ruins unearthed during its construction. A myriad of beautification projects has resulted in the renovation of many of the city's landmark buildings. This renaissance has not been merely cosmetic, and Athens has become cleaner and greener with the restoration of parks and squares and the creation of newly pedestrianized areas that unify the major archaeological sites in the city centre. The legacy of the Olympics has been a new sense of civic pride and a renewed self-confidence and optimism, forging a positive image of Athens as a modern European capital.

In his oration for the dead during the Peloponnesian War, Pericles equated human happiness with freedom. The political freedom which made Athens famous as the birthplace of democracy extends to the present day, manifestated in the freedom from fear; Athens has the lowest crime rate in Europe and is one of the safest cities in the world. Greeks are disdainful of constraints upon their natural spontaneity and like being able to come and go as they please, buying tickets for a serendipitous getaway to the islands minutes before departure. Freedom is also extended to four-legged companions, and the city's numerous stray cats and dogs can be seen about town making regular appearances in the local taverns and using crosswalks alongside human pedestrians. Although Athens can be characterized as a vast metropolis, it is still a village at heart. Only the inheritors of such intimate images such as the goddess of victory Nike adjusting her sandal (a sculpture in the Acropolis Museum) could create a city governed by maxims like 'man is the measure of all things'. In this way Athens differentiates itself from the grandeur and opulence of other European capitals. Whether you are in search of luxurious hotels, world-class gastronomic destinations, or the newest designer shop, or perhaps a solitary stroll in the Ancient Agora (see p. 54) or an all-night dance party, Athens has something for you. It is a city full of surprises, where turning a corner can lead you from a derelict building to a cluster of lively restaurant-bars and cafés.

Withstanding countless invasions, both ancient and modern, Athens has emerged from the ashes. The city is like a great poem or novel to which one returns with nostalgia, longing to experience it again as if for the first time. From Kifissia to Piraeus, residents and visitors alike continue to discover Athens anew, a continually changing, perplexing and enchanting place bathed in a light that elevates even its most undistinguished features. To submit to her charms is to join in a veritable conspiracy for pleasure, inventing your own Athens as you go off the beaten track, embarking on a journey sure to inspire what Athenian poet Odysseus Elytis, winner of the 1979 Nobel Prize for Literature, described as a 'love story with godlike dimensions'.

Street Wise

Psychiko • Halandri • Kifissia • Ekali • Kolonaki •
Syntagma • Plaka • Monastiraki • Thisio • Omonia • Gazi •
Psyrri • Glyfada • Vouliagmeni • Voula • Piraeus

Psychiko
Halandri
Kifissia
Ekali

Surrounded by Mt Penteli to the north, the Tourkovounia mountains to the west, and Mt Hymettos to the east, the northern suburbs offer greener, shadier neighbourhoods and a cooler climate than do other areas of the city. Mt Penteli is an attractive place for quiet walks along well-marked footpaths, taking strollers past the Monastery of Moni Pentelis and several traditional tavernas that are the bane of vegetarians. Life in the northern suburbs is at a more relaxed pace than in the city centre; the area was in fact countryside before the urban sprawl reached Kifissia, formerly an aristocratic retreat where wealthy Athenians built their summer homes. At the heart of Kifissia lies a thriving commercial centre, with upscale boutiques catering to the affluent residents of the north and linked by railway to the port of Piraeus in the south. The journey from end to end takes approximately one hour, and passes directly through the city centre en route.

Another popular district with lively café-bars and restaurants lies off Kefalari Square, providing a good place to relax after a hard day of shopping and museum-hopping between the Gaia Centre (see p. 20) and the Goulandris Museum of Natural History (see p. 20). Take a pleasant stroll around the neighbourhood, and admire the elegant 19th-century villas that line the leafy streets of the suburb. The houses may be highbrow, but the atmosphere is low-key and ideal for relaxing, exploring and shopping. Further up is the even more sparsely populated and exclusive neighbourhood of Ekali, while Maroussi is home to the impressively expanded, albeit controversial (how much did it cost?), Athens Olympics Sports Complex, redesigned by Spanish architect and engineer Santiago Calatrava, along with the future International Museum of Athletics, to be housed in the former International Broadcasting Centre.

Halandri to the south is more commercial and less engaging, but nevertheless full of wonderful shops of every variety, including patisseries that in themselves are worth the trip. Neo Psychiko, home of the progressive and groundbreaking Deste Foundation (see p. 17) for contemporary art and several embassies across the way, is dotted with small parks and squares, along with a few good eateries frequented by the neighbourhood's locals. The hotels in the northern suburbs are an oasis far from the hectic pace of the Athens city centre, with designer interiors and luxurious service that anticipates your every whim before you think of it.

The bright and charming ambiance of this quaint restaurant with its chilli-pepper-red walls and white floors of painted pine, pomegranate light fixtures and traditional wicker chairs promises the same warmth and simplicity in its dishes. Set in a residential area, this no-frills restaurant is clearly aimed at locals, and serves up fresh seafood at reasonable prices to a background of contemporary Greek music. The grilled crayfish are so succulent that any addition to their buttery richness would only detract from the perfection of their delicate flavour. Selections may be few, but whatever is on offer is guaranteed to be the best seafood around. For a taste of Greece in one mouthful, try the sea urchin marinated in olive oil and lemon.

In 1982, Stelios Parliaros started a revolution in Greek sweets when he began using strictly fresh ingredients in all his wares, hence the name 'Fresh'. Here you will find fine pastries, often beautifully decorated with extravagant designs made from fruit, along with unique desserts with surprising flavour combinations such as lavender, rosemary and mint, ice creams and Kayak sorbets flavoured with roses and Champagne, decadent Valrhona chocolates, and home-made preserves from bergamot to sour cherry. Sweets delightfully packaged in little bijoux boxes or displayed on colourful 'love platters' make ideal gifts, as do the books (which are also easier on the waistline) on gourmet desserts, wine, and art and design. Other branches are in Kolonaki and Glyfada.

Deste means 'to see', but in the realm of contemporary art it also means the place to be to view the latest and greatest. Founded by art collector Dakis Joannou in 1983, the Deste Foundation has no permanent collection, but serves as a vital bridge between the local and international art scenes by organizing significant exhibitions devoted to contemporary art. The latest of these, 'Monument to Now', coincided with the 2004 Summer Olympics and featured Joannou's extensive private collection, with works by Marcel Duchamp, Jeff Koons, Jenny Holzer, Barbara Kruger and Andy Warhol, to name a few. Located in a former paper warehouse, the unadorned framework has been retained and renovated to provide the exhibition space with state-of-the-art facilities. The foundation avoids the stultifying feeling of a formal museum by offering free admission and refreshment at chic bar-restaurant Cosmos (see p. 121).

Athens' most highly acclaimed hair salon owes its reputation to the talent of owner Vangelis Hadzis. One of the few super-successful individuals who has no desire to franchise or exploit his fame, Hadzis stands apart in his individual approach to his clients, whom he observes in much the same way as a portrait painter assesses his sitter. Noting the client's features and personality, Hadzis creates a personalized cut and style that offers more than a mere repetition of the latest fleeting trend. The entire affair is a unique experience, from the spacious interior designed by architect Babis Ioannou, to the pampering service of the beautiful assistants serving cappuccinos. Having the good fortune to get an appointment is quite another matter, as Hadzis is much sought after by Athenians-in-the-know. Book well in advance.

8 Palia Agora

26 Kehagia & M. Renieri

A central meeting place since the 1930s, Palia Agora, or 'old market', is the only café-bar in the affluent neighbourhood of Filothei. In warmer months the open tree-lined courtyard buzzes throughout the day with stylishly clad residents and movers-and-shakers from the nearby offices. The late afternoon and early evening hours see the arrival of the well-heeled 30-somethings of the northern suburbs for cocktails, burgers, snacks and salads. During the winter when the action moves indoors, the atmosphere becomes increasingly boisterous late into the night. The coffee is excellent and the Margaritas are possibly the best in town.

AESOP AND AGIORGITIKO

9 Tzitzikas & Mermigas

26 Eschylou & Agiou Giorgiou

With a name inspired by one of Aesop's fables, Tzitzikas ('ant') & Mermigas ('grasshopper') is a classic Greek taverna with a traditional deli-like atmosphere. Under a wood-beamed ceiling, jars of herbs and spices and bottles of *tsikoudia* and olive oil adorn the shelves. It is best to share lots of small dishes in order to sample as many flavours as possible, beginning with the less frequently encountered spinach and smoked-pork-stuffed onion baked in the oven, wild greens (*saganaki*) flambéed with a piquant cheese, or crispy golden tomato fritters. All should be enjoyed with the freely flowing barrel wine – either a red Agiorgitiko from the Nemea region, or the white Moschofilero from Mandinea, both balanced and full-bodied wines from the Peloponnesus.

THE BEST OF CRETE

10 Krisa Gi

23 Agiou Konstantinou

You don't have to travel all the way to Crete to experience authentic Cretan cuisine when Athens' very own Krisa Gi in Maroussi is serving up dishes made from ingredients imported straight from the island's organic farmlands. Black-and-white photographs of Cretan peasants, their toil deeply etched in the lines of their faces, adorn the dusky plum walls and create an evocative atmosphere of heritage. You will find all the traditional fare, from hand-made phyllo pies stuffed with wild greens and herbs, soft goat's cheese or onions, to the classic rusk bread topped with diced tomatoes, *anthotyro* cheese and capers, and doused with olive oil. The *apaki*, smoked pork sautéed in

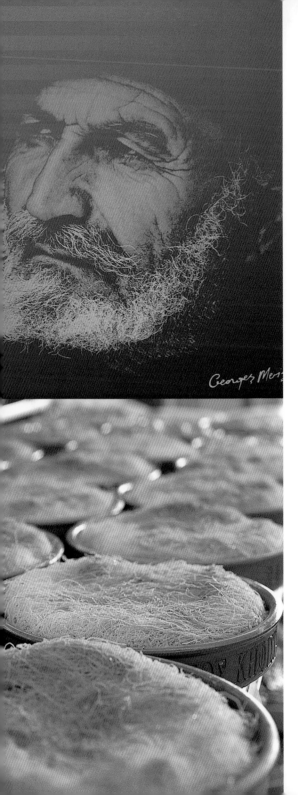

Georges Me[...]

a mélange of herbs, is extraordinary, as is the delicately flavoured rabbit baked in a yogurt sauce. Accompany your meal with one of the excellent Cretan wines on offer, such as Xerolithia made from Vilana grapes, or try the local spirit, *raki*.

PUPPET SHOW
11 Spathario Museum of Shadow Theatre
Vassilissis Sofias & D. Ralli, Kastalias Square

This unique and enchanting museum pays tribute to the history and art of the folk tradition of shadow-puppet theatre. Founded by one of the genre's greatest artists and performers Eugenios Spatharios, the collection of puppets (made by Spatharios himself) takes the visitor on a journey through the magical world of the popular hero, Karagiozis, who has delighted generations of Greeks since he first arrived from the east in the late 19th century. A long-armed eternal underdog whose wily ways get him in and out of mischief, Karagiozis, along with a colourful cast of characters drawn from Greek history and mythology, 'reflects the soul and spirit of the people'. Housed in a neoclassical mansion in Maroussi, the entertaining and inspiring collection presents a humourous approach to life's troubles.

BAKLAVA IN KIFISSIA
12 Varsos Kifissia
5 Kassaveti

The Varsos family has run this patisserie and dairy shop for over 110 years, and a visit to Varsos is a step (or rather several steps) back in time. The décor dates from the 1950s, when the second generation took over the business. In an age when products are loaded with preservatives and synthetic flavours, it is easy to recognize what distinguishes Varsos. Deciding what to try from the enormous range of sweets is no easy task. Choices run the gamut of traditional Greek pastries, from *baklava*, made from layers of phyllo pastry lined with walnuts, cinnamon and butter and drenched with warm honey, and *galaktoboureko*, a rich milk-custard pie, to the sublime *ek mek*, made of shredded phyllo rolled in pistachios and honey, and covered with cream. For something more merciful on the waistline, try the deliciously tart and creamy yogurt, served with one of the many fruit preserves.

It is an extraordinary pleasure to linger among the lions and tigers and bears (oh my!) at the Goulandris Museum of Natural History, and see the wide-eyed wonder on children's faces as they roam among the creatures on display. In addition to the collection, preservation, exhibition and study of plants, animals and minerals, the museum, founded in the 1960s by Angelos and Niki Goulandris, also strives to raise public awareness about the environment and the perils it faces. Today the museum's specimens number in the hundreds of thousands, including insects, mammals, birds, reptiles, shells, rocks, minerals and fossils from all over Greece. The botanical collection is especially impressive with over 200,000 species of plants, among which 145 have been recently discovered by the museum's own researchers. This remarkable collection is housed in an elegant villa, along with the Anemones coffee shop and a gift shop that sells Hermès scarves and porcelain plates designed by Niki Goulandris, as well as many of the museum's own publications.

The Goulandris Museum of Natural History (see above) opened its new centre for environmental research and education, the Gaia (Earth) Centre, in 2001. Unlike most museums that frown on touching the displays, the centre encourages visitors, particularly children, to interact with the exhibits in order to create a better understanding of the problems and possible solutions involved in environmental issues. The exhibition begins with displays concerning the Earth's systems and how they function, moving on to explore how humans have utilized its natural resources and to suggest more environmentally friendly ways of doing so. Unique to the museum is a hemispherical dome, the 'Geosphere', with a screen almost two stories high upon which digital images of the planet are projected, accompanied by music. Images of mankind's achievements are shown, alongside those of war and pollution. This review of history ends with the insistence of the pressing need to modify human behaviour to create a more harmonious relationship between man and nature.

In Greek, the word *berdema* is slang for 'entanglement'. In the kitchen of proprietor Pericles Fotiadis, the term refers to the restaurant's serendipitous fusion of eastern and western cuisines, reflecting far-reaching cultural entanglements that stretch back to Constantinople. In this modern taverna, with its casual atmosphere and playful décor, a thousand years of turbulent history dissolve into a lively mélange of flavours that transports you beyond borders. Dishes include *dolmades galantzi* (vine leaves stuffed with rice in yogurt), spicy feta pies made with phyllo pastry, and various renditions of the classic kebab, including *gelik* (minced beef filled with *graviera* goat's cheese, peppers and tomatoes). The region is also famous for its honey-drenched sweets, so be sure to leave room for something truly decadent, such as *kazanitipi*.

22 Prytaneion

37 Kolokotroni, Kefalari Square

In the middle of leafy Kefalari Square, the artsy atmosphere of Prytaneion is hip enough to draw all age groups for coffee and drinks, and is as popular with the more youthful crowd as it is with suited-and-booted business types. If you come for a meal, bring an appetite large enough to accommodate the enormous portions of over 100 Mediterranean-inspired dishes. This lively restaurant is the perfect place in which to escape the summer heat under misting ceiling fans, or to retreat to from the winter cold, surrounded by works by contemporary Greek artists like Bernadaki, Pavlos, Moralis and Gaitis. The service is friendly and attentive without being obtrusive, and the setting is trendy and laid-back. Open all day, year round.

BEEFEATERS

23 Telemachus

19 Fragopoulou

Telemachus is the place for carnivores. Opened in 1938 by the present owner's grandfather as a deli (*mezedopolio*), the Tsiligris family quickly became known for having the best beef in town. Having drawn capacity crowds on any given night for over a decade, this neighbourhood taverna located under a colonnade of mulberry trees offers succulent spit-roasted pig and lamb, while cuts of beef and braids of offal are grilled over an open fire. For private functions there is the baronial dining room, complete with fireplace and adjacent to a wine cellar that houses a good selection of Greek wine, well suited to the meaty menu.

CHOCOLATE AND CHILLI

24 Irene

57 Thiseos

Up in the northernmost suburbs of Ekali lies a confectionery outpost that caters strictly to takeaway customers. The unpretentiousness of this establishment may make you wonder what all the fuss is about, but all doubts will melt away when you experience Irene Pappa's chocolate creations and fresh-to-order tortes. The recipes seem to hearken back through history to the Aztecs, who once mixed cocoa beans with pepper, vanilla, chilli, or cinnamon to produce bitter, spicy concoctions that are reflected in Irene's philosophy of blending flavours. It is certainly worth the trek for such a unique taste experience.

Most people don't think of fur and leather when they think of Greece's warm climate – or didn't, that is, until Theodosia Tziveli burst upon the fashion scene, winning international acclaim for her finely tailored designs. A native of northern Greece, which has a long association with the fur trade, she founded her own label and established herself alongside the most famous designers in the world. True to the adage 'never a prophet in one's own land', Tziveli made her name in Italy where she still lives and works, and continues to wow the fashion world by combining fur and leather with eye-catching colours in unexpected ways and liberating them from their traditional image. Her sexily chic and stylishly sporty pieces are irresistible any time of day.

The well-known fine-art restorer and dealer Stavros Mihalarias opened his newest gallery in a restored neoclassical building just off Kifissias Avenue. This beautiful mansion has been transformed into a multifaceted art space, spanning three levels and hung with museum-quality works for discerning art lovers to admire or acquire. The ground floor hosts exhibitions of contemporary Greek and international artists, while the first floor is reserved for the gallery's permanent collection of painting and sculpture from the late 19th and early 20th centuries, 16th- to 19th-century Byzantine icons, antiquities, and other objets d'art. Those interested in larger works can take a stroll through the sculpture garden outside. For less expensive items, visit the retail space in the basement, which features limited-edition etchings, prints and miniature sculptures.

One of the unique delights of summer evenings in Athens and an integral part of Greek culture is seeing a film in one of the many open-air cinemas. The first such cinema, established in 1919, was the Boboniera in Kifissia. Located in an enchanting walled garden, the seating area features canvas director's chairs with small tables for drinks and snacks. Your movie-going experience is heightened by the fragrant night air scented by the jasmine and gardenia bushes that line the garden. Showings begin when the stars appear around 9:00 p.m., with a second showing at 11:00. Films are shown in their original language with Greek subtitles.

The small family-run and -owned Harlaftis winery has been producing wine since 1935 in northern Attica, a region that has been famous for viniculture since ancient times. The estate, located at the foothills of Mt Pentelis in the tiny village of Stamata, just north of Athens, cultivates the Greek grape varieties Savatiano and Assyrtiko, as well as the more familiar Cabernet Sauvignon and Chardonnay. Keeping the family tradition alive, the estate is now run by the third generation of the Harlaftis family, who have implemented the latest state-of-the-art equipment to produce 41,000 bottles a year, all certified organic. Wine-lovers wanting to tour this quaint winery or its estate in Nemea (which produces red Agiorgitiko) must call ahead and book a day in advance.

Kolonaki

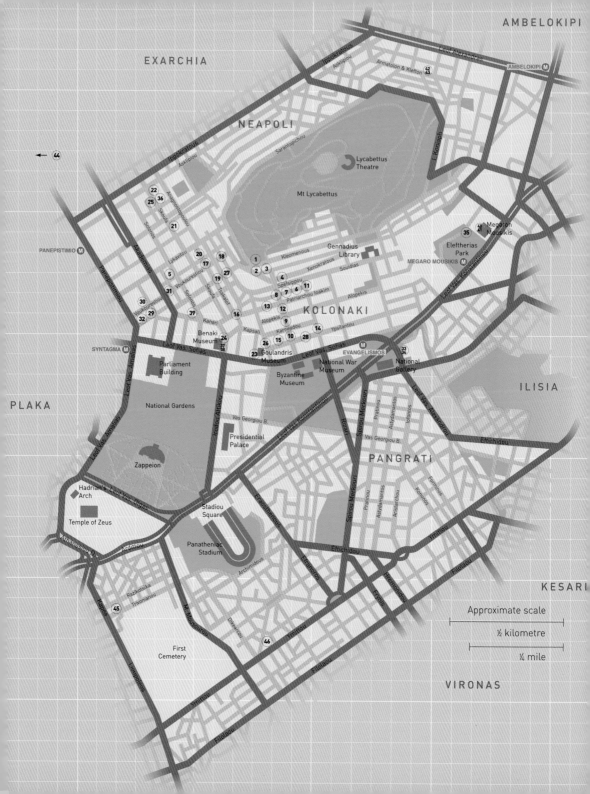

AMBELOKIPI

EXARCHIA

Insokratous

Askilpiou

Armatolon & Klefton 42
43

AMBELOKIPI Ⓜ

NEAPOLI

Sarantapichou

Ippokratous

Askilpiou

Lycabettus
Theatre

Mt Lycabettus

Leof. Konk

Megaron
Mousikis 40
41

Eleftherias
Park 35

PANEPISTIMIO Ⓜ

22
25 36

21

Kleomenous

Gennadius
Library

MEGARO MOUSIKIS Ⓜ

Leof. Vas. Konstantinou

Lykavitou

20

17

5

18

27

19

Skoufa

Voukourestiou

Tsakalof

1

2 3

4

Xenokratous

Souidias

Spelsippou

Alopekis

Patriarchou Ioakim

KOLONAKI

Leof. Vas. Sofias

Akademias

Sina

Omirou

Zalokosta

31

30
29

32

Voukourestiou

39

Kanari

16

Kapsali

13

12

8

15

9

26

7

10

6 11

Alopekis

Karneadou

28

14

Ypsilantou

23

Goulandris
Museum

Benaki
Museum 24
37

SYNTAGMA Ⓜ

Leof. Vas. Sofias

National War
Museum

EVANGELISMOS Ⓜ

33
34

National
Gallery

ILISIA

Parliament
Building

Byzantine
Museum

PLAKA

National Gardens

Troias Athikou

Vas Georgiou B.

Leof. Vas. Konstantinou

Rigillis

Spirou Merkouri

Pratinou

Astidamantos

Efantos

Vas Georgiou B.

PANGRATI

Eftichidou

Presidential
Palace

Leof. Vas. Amalias

Zappeion

Hadrian's
Arch

Leof. Vas. Olgas

Temple of Zeus

Stadiou
Square

Panathenaic
Stadium

Archimidous

Markou Mousourou

Diakou

Papadiamanta

Eftanisson

Eratosthenous

Eftichidou

Spirou Merkouri

Pratinou

Astidamantos

Aristarchou

Konnou

Froninis

Imittou

Filolaou

KESARI

First
Cemetery

Kallisperi

Kallirrois

Rasikotsika

Trivonianou

45

46

Ymittou

Filolaou

Approximate scale

½ kilometre

¼ mile

Laupheus

Ymittou

Filolaou

VIRONAS

44

Undoubtedly the most sophisticated fashion district of Athens, Kolonaki, with its designer boutiques and sophisticated galleries, is always buzzing. Platea Filikis Eterias, the neighbourhood's central square, boasts lively and stylish cafés, each with its own group of devoted regulars who hold court with friends and get on with the serious business of people-watching and the national pastime of talking politics. Kolonaki attracts trendy youth, kolonakiotes (residents who consider themselves citizens of their neighbourhood first and of Athens second, a phenomenon not exclusive to Kolonaki), intellectuals, politicians, and various glitterati and their entourages.

As Kolonaki is removed from the ancient sites, it is relatively free from tourists and provides an authentic glimpse into Athenian daily life, albeit a more conspicuously affluent one. One of the most exclusive addresses in the area is Haritos, a tiny street of enormous prestige on which can be found excellent galleries and eateries and the latest in boutique hotels. Skoufa is ideal for stopping in at the many stylish bars and cafés, while Patriarchou Ioakim, which runs through the centre of Kolonaki, is best for window shopping, as is Tsakalof with its tempting jewelry stores. The designer-friendly streets of Valaoritou and Voukourestiou could be mistaken for Paris's Rue de St Honoré-Faubourg or New York's Fifth Avenue. Saunter through snobbish Millione, a pedestrianized area with trendy restaurants, or flex your Gold Card at the designer shops lining Ploutarchou and Loukianou, which lead down to the main avenue of Vassilissis Sofias and 'Museum Row'.

Once you've had your fill of the Kolonaki scene, head up to Athens' highest point, Mt Lycabettus, for spectacular views of the city. If you are feeling energetic, make the steep 45-minute climb up one of the paths leading to the tiny chapel of St George, perched on the summit, or take the easy way up via the funicular. At the top is a pricey café and restaurant of uncertain quality; ownership changes from private to state ownership at irregular intervals, but it just may be worth a visit for the memorable views. Upon descending from the Olympian heights, stop in at the superb Gennadeion Library, named after a Greek diplomat and bibliophile who donated his entire collection of illuminated manuscripts and over 27,000 rare books to the American School of Classical Studies. Above the entrance are inscribed the words of Isocrates: 'They are called Greeks who share in our culture.' A five-minute walk will take you to some of the finest museums in the city, including the Benaki Museum (see p. 40) and its superb café (see. p. 121); the Goulandris Museum of Cycladic Art (see p. 34), the Byzantine Museum and the National War Museum, with the National Gallery a little further along Vassilissis Sofias.

The name reveals the unconventional opening hours (3:00 to 11:00 p.m.) of this eccentric shop featuring the best in Greek fashion. Part of the St George Lycabettus hotel (see p. 92) in Kolonaki, this winsome space (located next to hip bar-restaurant Frame; see p. 128) showcases the latest chic and funky styles for both men and women, displayed as individual works of art in vintage wood-and-glass Art Déco cabinets. Stage designer Antonis Kalogridis is behind the look of the shop's interior, which undergoes a seasonal metamorphosis with new colour schemes and décor to match the changing collections. As the country's most noteworthy designers are represented, it is the perfect place to see what's new on the Greek designer scene and to while away the afternoon.

Medusa's reputation does not stem from the well-known artists who have exhibited here, but rather from the now well-known artists who got their start here before becoming famous, thanks to the intuition of owner Maria Dimitriadis. For over 20 years her ability to recognize budding talent and to juxtapose the established with the up-and-coming has been vital in keeping Medusa on the front line of the Athens art scene. Exhibited works have been described by the owner as 'experimental', 'youthful' and 'questing', revealing an intuitive approach to curatorship, rather than one based in history and theory. At Medusa you can enjoy the experience of seeing tomorrow's talent today, without the risk of turning into stone.

Specializing in Greek antiques, Goutis is brimful of cultural artefacts, some dating to the Byzantine Empire. Perusing this splendid collection is like a journey back through country's long history. You will find a bit of everything here, including jewelry, textiles, books, furniture, icons, weaponry, sculpture, paintings, and even examples of traditional costumes from all over Greece. Owner Giorgos Goutis, who is also president of the Hellenic Association of Antiquarians & Art Dealers, took over the business from his father Stavros, who started it in the 1930s. Each piece has a story to tell, often one that Mr Goutis is willing to share, revealing something about the people and times that produced it. Goutis is a significant collection that is as much a cultural experience as it is a commercial one.

Marianna Petridi began organizing annual solo exhibitions out of her own workshop more than 20 years ago, and it wasn't long before the space grew into one of Athens' foremost exhibition venues, presenting the work of Greece's most talented young jewelry designers. This quaint little boutique showcases each designer's pieces in separate display cabinets, allowing you to survey a diversity of styles that defies categorization. You will also find Petridi's own gold and jeweled creations, as well as colourful faux bijoux made from every imaginable material, from vintage objects from the Twenties and Thirties to semiprecious stones, glass, beads, and even old postage stamps. Many of the pieces are one-off, with prices ranging from inexpensive to high end.

11 Ratka

30–32 Haritos

Always crowded and buzzing, Ratka is one of those places that manages to remain fashionable without any distinguishing features to explain its ultra-chic status. Ask the owner her secret and she shrugs with a mischievous smile as she surveys the tide of devotees who flock to her restaurant. Bulgarian-born Ratka has been hosting an anarchic mix of the Athenian élite for over 30 years. The place is something of a cross between a bistro and a bar-restaurant, with a menu that features everything from snails to sushi. Come for the atmosphere if you enjoy seeing who's who and try the specialty of the house, spaghetti with *avgotaraho* (also known as *bottarga*, a pungent fish roe that is pressed and preserved in wax), which is outrageously delicious.

PURE AND SIMPLE

12 To Kafenio

26 Loukianou

These days when the love affair with fusion cooking shows no signs of abating, it is refreshing to find unadulterated Greek cuisine alive and well in this classic Kolonaki establishment. For 20 years purists have applauded Elly Theodoridou's perfect and simple recipes, and the opportunity to enjoy home cooking in an elegant atmosphere. Diners may find their eyes straying to the wood panelling dotted with framed place settings, to make out the scribblings and signatures of the many famous personalities who have passed through To Kafenio's doors. Specialties include the house salad with diced courgettes, spring onions, artichokes, mushrooms and green beans in a light lemon and dill dressing; melt-in-your-mouth stuffed cabbage leaves in an egg lemon sauce; and cuttlefish with spinach.

ECCENTRIC NATURE

13 Fanourakis

139

HATS OFF

14 Planet Earth

137

MEZE MECCA

15 To Ouzadiko

110

Konstantinos Nomicos and Eleni Meladini have been designing minimalist furniture since the beginning of their careers in the 1960s. Fashioned exclusively from wood, the craftsmanship and simplicity of the designs have placed them firmly in the realm of timeless classics. Despite its distinctive look, the furniture blends harmoniously with any décor, from refined to rustic, traditional to modern, and has featured in stylish Athenian homes for over 30 years. Opus's pieces are made from the highest quality materials available and combine different textures and colours, and can be made-to-order in any type of wood, in any size or shape. Acquiring one of these designs can be likened to owning a family heirloom, which is inevitably what it will become.

Having established their reputation on the island of Paros, Argyro and Manoli have recently become the newest addition to the Kolonaki culinary scene, bringing with them their signature dish of octopus slow-cooked in Vinsanto and honey over crispy potatoes. A small display of the goods on offer, including unusual local shellfish, lets you choose from the fresh catch of the day. Other dishes, such as risotto with scallops, langoustines and spinach, and vegetarian linguine with artichoke hearts and parmesan, are also highly recommended. Desserts are creative renditions of classics like *moustalevria* made from grapes scented with mastic, or the chocolate *kormos* made with chestnuts. Papadakis also offers an excellent selection of after-dinner spirits from grappa and cognac, to *tsipouro* and sweet wines for the perfect finish.

This unassuming café has a long history as a neighbourhood hangout. Located on the well-trodden Skoufa Street, it became the haunt of the intelligentsia and film and theatre crowd over the years. Visually it has little to recommend it, but has that unmistakably homey feeling that encourages lingering over coffee and the morning papers, chatting with friends and people-watching. The coffee is rich and delicious, and the service friendly in this lively, yet laid-back café, where the regular clientele come and go throughout the day. The amiable Nezi sisters, who own and run Filion, also serve light lunches and traditional pastries made from family recipes, along with over 20 flavours of Kayak, the famous Greek ice-cream brand.

A congenial meeting place for post-shopping sprees or pre-dinner cocktails, this café-bar attracts a stylish crowd. Chic women and trendy men-about-town lounge on sofas inside, or venture outside to the pillow-lined sidewalk. The minimalist and contemporary décor, with its appealing mix of cream with shades of green and chocolatey-brown, makes En Delphis a popular venue with the fashion-conscious set. Chill-out music sets the scene for relaxing and enjoying a coffee or specialty Daiquiri.

Spanning the period from 5000 to 2000 BC, the museum's collection of Cycladic art, donated by Nikoloas and Ekaterini Goulandris, is one of the most comprehensive of its kind. The minimalist marble building, designed by Ioannis Vikelas, is well suited to the aesthetic of the collection, which features the familiar marble figurines whose exquisite simplicity inspired such 20th-century artists as Modigliani. A glass corridor joins the modern building to the 19th-century Stathatos Mansion, which hosts the museum's temporary exhibitions. Designed by Bavarian architect Ernest Ziller, it is one of the best examples of neoclassical architecture in Athens. The museum also has a café and gift shop carrying books, educational games, and items inspired by Cycladic art.

NO-WORRIES BEADS

24 Kombologadiko

6 Koumbari

Not to be confused with a rosary, the Greek *komboloy* exists purely for pleasure and contemplation. Although many theories exist regarding its origin, one thing is certain – if you are in the market for one you are sure to find something to suit your taste among the hundreds on display at Kombologadiko. *Komboloys* can be made from a variety of materials, including semiprecious stones, bone, horn, glass, coral, and the traditional amber. The size and number of beads also varies, but it is generally agreed that they should be strung on a silk cord, rather than a chain, for better gliding and to enhance acoustical and tactile enjoyment. The friendly staff of Kombologadiko can also customize anything you wish on the premises, where you will find *komboloys* ranging in price from €10 to €10,000. It is worth a stop, if just for the visual delight.

SILVER AND GOLD

25 Kariofillis

1 Staikou

Emilios Kariofillis is a jeweler who designs, produces and sells his own work exclusively out of his tiny atelier in Kolonaki. A native of the Epirus region in northern Greece, famous for its hand-made silver and metal folk crafts, Kariofillis decided at an early age to follow in his father's footsteps as a jewelry designer. Having experimented with a range of materials and methods, today he works mainly in 18- and 22-karat gold and semiprecious stones. His style is reminiscent of the ancient Greek and Byzantine periods, but also exhibits a decidedly contemporary flair. Often employing ancient methods, such as the lost-wax technique, Kariofillis creates limited editions as well as one-of-a-kind pieces, all of which bear the unmistakable hand of an accomplished and experienced goldsmith.

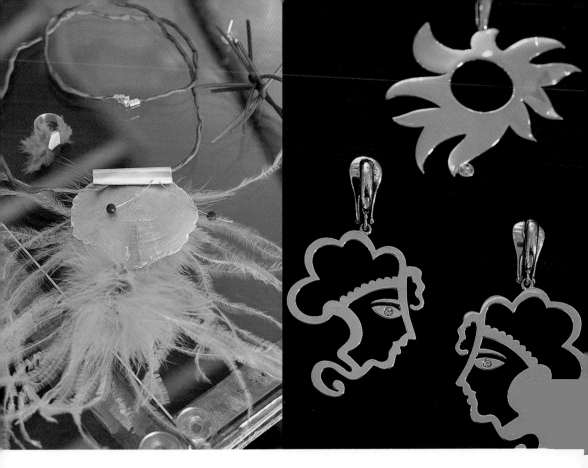

26 Astrolavos Artlife

11 Irodotou

27 Liana Vourakis

42 Pindarou

Antonia Dimitrakopoulou has been an art dealer for many years, and has hosted some of the biggest names in the world of contemporary art. In opening Astrolavos Artlife down the street from her other high-profile gallery, Astrolavos Dexameni, Dimitrakopoulou had a different aim in mind, specifically to make art more people-friendly and attainable to a wider consumer public. This idea of approaching art through more accessible objets d'art, some with everyday uses, is ideal for those looking for a unique and personal – as well as reasonably priced – gift. Works come from the studios of over 70 Greek artists, in all shapes, sizes and media. The gallery also hosts temporary exhibitions every month.

While Liana Vourakis's designs draw on tradition, they are anything but traditional. With originality and finesse, she uses the power of symbols to create decorative household objects, jewelry and good-luck charms that radiate positive energy. Working with such familiar Greek motifs as the national flag, the traditional pom-pom shoes of the *Evzones*, the evil eye, garlic and pomegranates, Vourakis uses a range of materials and colours to transform these themes into a sophisticated style that is all her own. Although her inspiration draws from such Greek sources as Minoan frescos and 19th-century embroideries, her works take on surprisingly novel forms, from silver butterfly crowns to Limoges ashtrays. Her imitators are numerous, but there is only one Vourakis, whose feel-good lifestyle shop is full of eminently covetable objects.

28 Cava Anthidis
13-15 Ypsilantou

In today's global market where most things, from French foie gras to Ethiopian coffee, are readily available, Greek wines are still very hard to find abroad. This is due in part to the small production; there are approximately 250 producers and 1,200 labels, of which only 15 per cent is exported. At Cava Anthidis, you will find most of these and much more, as it carries the largest and most comprehensive selection of wine and spirits in the country, including over 5,000 labels of wine, 200 single malts, and 100 Champagnes. Besides having an extensive selection of international vintages, Cava Anthidis is the only wine merchant to carry a significant selection of Greek labels, affording the opportunity to see the development of the country's wines over time.

TAILOR MADE
29 Harris & Angelos
18 Voukourestiou

This internationally acclaimed duo creates some of the most sought-after items of haute couture in Greece. Specializing in women's formal wear, Harris & Angelos' hand-made garments are characterized by their elegant and simple lines and are created with careful attention to the smallest detail. The textures and colours are unique and sensuous, and the designs enhance the silhouette and express the femininity of the female form. Women look (and feel) ravishing when wearing Harris & Angelos' designs, which are made-to-order in any size or colour. Only for the fortunate...

PERFECT POTTERY
30 ADC Eleni Vernadaki
133

JEWELRY WITH A TWIST
31 Pentheroudakis
19 Voukourestiou

A promenade down Voukourestiou, Kolonaki's most exclusive (and expensive) street, will lead you to Pentheroudakis, which has been supplying fine jewelry for over 50 years. Initially browsers will be drawn to the eye-catching window display featuring unique designs by well-known Greek artists, and once inside, will discover marvellous pieces that have drawn on tradition as a valuable source of inspiration and combined it with a contemporary twist in their designs. Known as the jeweler of choice for Athenian ladies because of the quality and reasonable prices, Pentheroudakis continues its legacy of superior craftsmanship.

ROYAL DELI
32 Cava Cellier
31 Patriarchou Ioakim

When Cava Cellier opened in 1938, the store supplied the Athenian aristocracy and royalty with the most exclusive delicatessen products available at the time. Pavlos Karakostas continues his family's legacy by providing the city with a comprehensive selection of wine and Champagne from all over the world. Cava Cellier also offers a wide variety of Greek wine and spirits, including its own label, Montofoli. Made of four grape varieties indigenous to the Aegean and cultivated on the island of Evia, Montofoli continues a tradition of sun-dried sweet wines dating back to ancient times. Those interested in Greek viniculture can learn more by attending one of the shop's tastings and discover some of the country's emerging world-class wines.

ATHENS VIA MANHATTAN
33 Milos
107

RUM WITH A VIEW
34 Galaxy Bar (Hilton)
127

PARKLIFE
35 The Park Restaurant
Eleftherias Park, Vassilissis Sofias

A statue of prominent Greek statesman Venizelos keeps watch over this well-kept secret, tucked away in Eleftherias Park. The Park Restaurant, frequented only by Athenians-in-the-know, serves Greek fare from a menu that changes daily and reflects influences from around the world. Due to its proximity to the embassies, hospital and the Athens Concert Hall (see p. 40), much of the Park's clientele are diplomats, doctors and concert-goers. During the day, you'll find a lovely sunlit café set amongst the eucalyptus and shady plane trees, while at night the scene changes to a quiet romantic restaurant, with an adjoining bar for those seeking a livelier setting for tête-à- tête cocktails.

This small, intimate bookshop carries books on fine art, photography, architecture and theatre, as well as illustrated books about Greece from Koan Publishing House. The stock is primarily English-language editions, but there is also a selection of publications in other languages. Coffee and comfortable chairs are provided, giving this unique shop the unhurried feel of a library.

Housed in a neoclassical mansion across from the National Gardens (see p. 46), the museum was founded by art collector Antoni Benaki in 1931. Exhibits are organized chronologically, from prehistoric and ancient Greece, through to the Roman era and medieval Byzantium. Other floors offer political and cultural glimpses into the country's history, from the fall of Constantinople (1453) to the formation of the Greek state after the War of Independence (1832). On display are textiles, costumes, weaponry, and two period rooms reconstructed from an Ottoman mansion in northern Greece. After swotting up on your Greek history, venture upstairs to the roof garden for a bite to eat at the museum's first-rate café restaurant (see p.121)

Hosting opera, ballet, symphony and theatre performances during its October–June season, the Athens Concert Hall is one of the largest cultural centres in the world and is renowned for its superb acoustics. The Hall of the Friends of Music can accommodate up to 2,000 concert-goers; more intimate spaces include the Dimitris Mitropoulos Hall, the Alexandra Trianti Hall, and the Nicos Skalkotas Hall. An expansion in 2004 provided space for exhibition areas, shops and restaurants, and a music library.

While its future home in the old Fix brewery is being renovated (opening in 2007), the National Museum of Contemporary Art has taken up residence in the new wing of the Athens Concert Hall. Established in 2000, the museum's permanent collection comprises works of painting, sculpture, video, 'experimental architecture' and photography. Past exhibitions have included such names as Jannis Kounellis, Kim Sooja, Costas Tsoclis and Rebecca Horn, and a large retrospective devoted to Greek artists of the 1970s is planned for 2006. Originally built in 1863 but abandoned since the 1970s, the brewery is being transformed by a new team of architects. The arrival of a permanent museum will be an exciting (if long overdue) feature of the city's contemporary art scene.

When the Ileana Tounta gallery opened in 1988, it was the first such space of its kind in Athens. Located in a former print factory, the building was renovated in 2003 by architects Katerina Diakomedou and Nikos Charitos, who preserved much of the structure's industrial character. The centre houses the stylish 48 The Restaurant (see p. 108), an excellent bookshop, and two expansive exhibition areas. Specializing in alternative and innovative art, it is also one of the few galleries in the city that emphasizes photographic exhibitions.

Syntagma
Plaka
Monastiraki
Thisio

Syntagma ('Constitution') Square is the historic centre of Athens. Here you will find the 1842 Parliament Building along with the Evzones in their traditional kilted costume, who put on a ceremonial changing of the guard every hour at the Tomb of the Unknown Soldier. Head for the National Gardens (see p. 46) for a picnic or afternoon walk, or stroll past the Zappeion Gardens and catch an evening film at open-air cinema Aegli (see p. 124). Nearby is 'Kallimarmaro' (or 'beautiful marble'), rebuilt on the site of the ancient Panathinaiko Stadium to host the first modern Olympics in 1896. The main streets in the area are Ermou, Athens' main shopping street; Akadimias, leading from Kolonaki and home to the Numismatic Museum; and Panepistimiou, lined with beautiful neoclassical buildings that house the University of Athens, the Academy of Arts and the National Library. Other major avenues include Stadiou, leading to Omonia Square; Leof Vassilissis Amalias, which passes Hadrian's Arch; and Vassilissis Sofias, heading up towards the northern suburbs.

One of the most rewarding places in which to while away an afternoon is the Ancient Agora (see p. 54), or 'marketplace', once the centre of Athenian life. Walk in the footsteps of philosophers and politicians along the colonnaded Stoa of Attalos, now a museum devoted to Athenian democracy, towards the wonderfully preserved Temple of Hephaestus. Excellent cafés and *mezedopolia* are nearby when it's time for a rest. The local monuments are too numerous to mention, and every stone has a story to tell. In the shadow of the Acropolis is the historic neighbourhood of Plaka, with its romantic cobbled streets, jewelry shops, tavernas and kitsch souvenirs. Sit in Platea Filomouson for a coffee or *ouzo* break, or duck into the cool interior of Vrettos (see p. 52) for a *raki* in one of the area's oldest distillery bars. To fully appreciate Plaka, walk the length of Adrianou and stop off for *souvlaki* at Kostos; the sign above the tiny stall reads *ohi anhos* ('no stress'). Continue on to Monastiraki, where you can explore both upmarket and flea-market antique shops. It is also one of the few places in which to see remnants of the Turkish mosques that predate Greek independence.

If during your stroll you're still feeling peckish, try Athens' answer to fast food, the inexpensive and satisfying kebab. A more interesting route up to the Parthenon is the back way through the charming district of Anafiotika, built by refugees from Asia Minor. Plaka is full of many interesting small museums, including the folk, Jewish, musical instruments, Turkish baths and children's museums. Local Byzantine churches like Agios Nikolaos Rangavas (see p. 50) are worth a visit, and don't miss the opportunity to see an open-air performance at the Odeon of Herodes Atticus (see p. 49), a truly magical experience and one of the glories of a summer in Athens.

A WALK IN THE PARK
1 National Gardens
Irodou Attikou

Between the Parliament Building and Hadrian's Wall lie 40 acres of lushly verdant National Gardens, within which countless unexpected pleasures await discovery. Created at the behest of Queen Amalia in the 1830s, it is one of the most peaceful and enchanting places in the city for a quiet stroll. Winding paths lead past benches with languid lovers, towering palm trees, duck ponds, a small botanical museum, Roman mosaics, a tiny zoo, and statues of such illustrious figures as the philhellene Lord Byron and Greece's national poet, Dionysios Solomos. The garden's focal point is the impressive Zappeion Exhibition Hall, with its graceful neoclassical façade framed by Corinthian columns. The building was designed by Danish architect Theophilus Jansen in 1888 with an endowment from the Zappas cousins, whose statues may be seen on either side of the entrance. The city's first open-air cinema, Aegli (see p. 124), is located next door.

OUTDOOR ELEGANCE
2 Aegli + Lallabai
124

GREAT BRITON
3 Hotel Grande Bretagne
90

A PIECE OF THE PIE
4 Ariston
10 Voulis

Back in 1910, when Athens was still a village, a tiny shop opened in the centre of town serving just the one item for which it would become famous: *tiropita*, or feta cheese pie. So delicate was its crust, so creamy and flavourful its filling, that those with discerning palates bypassed the ubiquitous pies sold on every corner in favour of a *tiropita* from Ariston. Happily the tradition continues with even more passion and zest for quality from the new generation of the Lobotessi family, who continue to combine traditional ingredients with modern facilities to produce their wonderful *tiropitas*. More recently, the product line has expanded to include other pies, including spinach, leek, mushroom and chicken.

5 Hadzilias

21 Voulis

The traditional art of making clothes by hand may slowly be dying out with today's frenetic pace and consumer appetite for fleeting fashions and trends that change with the seasons. There are, however, always exceptional circumstances created by exceptional people, one of whom is Apostolis Hadzilias, who has been hand-tailoring suits with an artist's attention to detail since 1949. Apprenticed at the age of 13, Hadzilias has since become a master of his trade, and uses only the finest materials imported from all over Europe. With painstaking precision and exacting standards, he creates suits with an extraordinary fit that you will never tire of wearing.

PLUMS AND PISTACHIOS

6 Aristokratikon

9 Karagiorgi Servias

Aristokratikon, the city's finest confiserie, has been producing hand-made chocolates and sweets since 1928. Ever faithful to his secret family recipes, George Bitsopoulos has expanded the range over the years to include over 120 temptingly delicious goodies made with nuts, or flavoured with fruit, liqueur and cream. In a workshop at the base of Mt Lycabettus, a small team of technicians uses select Greek products, such as hand-picked plums from Skopelos, pistachios from Aegina, chestnuts from Pelion, and sour cherries from Tripoli to create sweets that are shipped fresh each day to Aristokratikon's two locations. This sweetshop is a chocoholic's dream, but be sure not to miss the sublime (and addictive) pistachio sticks.

FROM THE MASTIC TREE

7 Mastiha Shop

133

8 Korres
8 Ivikou & Eratosthenous

The Korres line of natural beauty care is the offspring of Athens' first homeopathic pharmacy, opened by George Korres in 1996. Exploiting the abundance of therapeutic plants indigenous to Greece, Korres has created a range of lotions and potions that contain only natural botanical ingredients to nourish your skin and hair. These luscious and deliciously fragrant products are a welcome alternative to the chemically-processed merchandise that pervades today's market. Eye creams made from jasmine and hibiscus, moisturizers of pomegranate and wild rose, basil-lemon and mint-tea body waters, vanilla and cinnamon shower gel, sage and nettle shampoo, and after-sun yogurt are but a few of the more than 150 scrumptious products available at Korres's various pharmacies around town, at the airport, in the Attica Centre on Panepistimiou, and, of course, this original pharmacy in Pangrati.

BIBLIOPHILIA
9 Eleftheroudakis
17 Panepistimiou

You will find everything from archaeology and philosophy to dictionaries and cookbooks at Eleftheroudakis, Athens' most comprehensive bookstore. Indulge in a serendipitous browse over the seven floors of English- and Greek-language publications, and pick up something for your travels or the obligatory phrase book to get you in and out of trouble. And what of all the gifts and souvenirs you must take back (if you go back)? At Eleftheroudakis you will find all of these, and more. The top floor also has a very good café sporting a tastefully minimalist décor that serves coffee and snacks. A must for all bibliophiles.

BOTTOMS UP
10 Galaxy
10 Stadiou

In front of the National Historical Museum (formerly the old Parliament Building) stands a bronze statue of Theodoros Kolokotronis, hero of the War of Independence, seated astride his horse and pointing the way to the Galaxy bar. Tucked away in an unassuming arcade off Panepistimiou, it is here that barflies of all lands unite. A long, narrow wood-panelled space lined with leather stools on either side makes for an intimate and cozy atmosphere in which experienced tipplers can take their pick from a wide variety of spirits. Attracting a diverse crowd of regulars from well-dressed businessmen to young bohemians, Galaxy is presided over by a gallery of such celebrated dipsomaniacal literary figures as Ernest Hemingway, Charles Bukowski and Jack Kerouac. One of the more charming places in town for the serious drinker.

ANCIENT AMPHITHEATRE
11 Odeon of Herodes Atticus
Dionisou Areopagitou

Herodes Atticus, benefactor and friend of the emperor Hadrian, built the amphitheatre that bears his name on the south slope of the Acropolis in memory of his wife, Aspasia Annia Regilla, in 161 AD. Restored in the 1950s, the theatre is used today for entertainment organized by the annual Athens Festival, and its tiers of Roman arches provide a spectacular backdrop for productions held by opera and ballet companies, orchestras and theatre troupes from all around the world. Maria Callas and Luciano Pavarotti (and Sting) are among the renowned singers who have graced the moonlit stage of the 5,000-seat Odeon, also known as the Herodion. Performances take place every evening in the summer.

GREEK GOODIES
12 Mesogaia
52 Nikis & Kydathineon

If you have ever been at the airport and noticed the bulging suitcases of nervously nonchalant passengers, they probably belong to ex-pat Greeks returning to their adopted homelands with as much local produce as possible. And their last port of call would undoubtedly have been Mesogaia, suppliers of traditional specialty foods from all over Greece. Here you will find fruity, peppery olive oil from Crete, rich cheese and hard rusk break, along with the local spirit, *raki*. Pick up some pungent Spartan herbs and wild mountain tea, fragrant honey from Kalamata, or preserves made from walnut (made while still green) or bergamot from Macedonia. Just make sure that you arrive at the store with a friend or two to help you carry all of your delicious purchases.

13 Frissiras Museum

3 & 7 Monis Asteriou

The Frissiras Museum is housed in two beautifully restored neoclassical buildings, located next door to one another in the heart of Plaka. Its founder Vlassis Frissiras began collecting works by contemporary artists in 1978, with an emphasis on depictions of the human form. The collection now contains over 2,000 paintings and 1,000 drawings, including works by David Hockney, Paula Rego, William Blake and Frank Auerbach, alongside such Greek artists as Nikos Kessanlis, Giannis Moralis and Costas Tsoclis, that chart the course of figurative painting in Europe. The museum organizes periodic exhibitions of major European artists, as well as an annual series of lectures. You will also find a lovely café and gift shop with original hand-made creations that are both decorative and utilitarian.

GLAMOURPUSS
14 Celia Kritharioti

8 Dedalou

Plunging necklines, discreet flashes of leg and hip-hugging silhouettes make Celia Kritharioti's bespoke creations both sexy and refined. Born into a fashion family, Kritharioti started designing at the age of 16 and began her career at the oldest haute couture house (established in 1906) in Greece. Upon acquiring the business in 1980, she brought a freshness and new life to the old company and now has three ateliers famous for embroidery that incorporates pearls, sequins, semiprecious stones and Swarovski crystals, and for garments that are each a work of art. Kritharioti, who insists that she likes designing for the curvaceous woman, has seen supermodels like Naomi Campbell and Claudia Schiffer sashay down the catwalk in her gorgeous gowns. An ever-growing waiting list of brides-to-be also await her designs as the last word in nuptial luxury.

A LITTLE LAMB
15 Taverna Xinos

4 Geronta

Tucked away off Plaka's main square, with its touristy shops and restaurants, is Taverna Xinos. Xinos, like his father before him, serves home-style fare, a family tradition for over 70 years. Everything is delicious, but the specialty of the house is lamb. Try it fricasseed with sautéed lettuce in an egg and lemon sauce, as a stew baked in clay pots

with pasta (*giouvetsi*), or just plain grilled. A strolling duo playing guitars serenades the crowd with popular Greek folk songs, and the house wine flows freely from the barrel. The cozy interior is decorated with murals of old Athens by Doris, a well-known artist of the 1950s, and the charming tree-lined courtyard is available for dining al fresco in the summer. At Taverna Xinos, the atmosphere is as authentically Greek as it gets.

BYZANTINE CHURCH
16 Agios Nikolaos Rangavas

1 Pritaniou

Located in the Rizocastro, the Byzantine heart of Plaka, stands this 11th-century cruciform church named for its benefactor. The dimly lit interior is perfumed by incense and adorned with glittering icons, most of which came from Russia in the 19th century. Remnants of Greece's pagan past are present in Christian guise, such as the sanctuary's altar, made from the capital of a Hellenistic column and incorporating the Corinthian acanthus and Egyptian lotus. The church is celebrated for its famous bell, whose tolling is said to have announced the start of the Greek revolution in 1821. Come after sunset for the beautiful Vespers service and an introduction to Greek Orthodox ritual in this architecturally, historically and spiritually fascinating building.

MILK PIES AND CRÊPES
17 Amalthia Galactopolio

16 Tripodon

Tripodon Street, once adorned with votive statues set up by tragedians who had won competitions for their plays, is alleged to be the oldest street in Greece. On this very avenue you will find the Amalthia *galactopolion*, modelled on old-fashioned shops that once supplied the neighbourhood with such dairy goods as home-made yogurt and milk pies. In winter, a wood-burning stove warms up a room decorated with frescos, marble-top tables and traditional wooden chairs. Order coffee served with a mini Ion chocolate, and sample the house specialty *galactoboureko*, milk pie drenched in honey. Amalthia also offers crèpes both savoury and sweet, a Greek take on a French classic.

18 Katerina Psoma

18 Pritaniou

The Stoic philosopher Epictetus held that one should discover what one truly is and become that thing. True to her own calling, Katerina Psoma came to create beautiful jewelry after an earlier career as an historian of Byzantine art. Her flair with materials found in London flea markets during her student days caught the attention of the Athenian fashion world, and it was not long before she was collaborating with boutiques both in Greece and abroad. Her pieces can be made of lace, wood, Venetian glass, silk, beads, and vintage Swarovski crystals, all arranged in intriguing and fanciful combinations. Psoma's style transforms with her ever-changing inspirations, resulting in original work that is vivacious and colourful, proving the proverb that art is indeed a revolt against fate.

19 Vrettos

41 Kydathineon

Vrettos is one of the oldest watering holes in historic Plaka, and has been serving and producing spirits on the premises for over 100 years. Revellers strolling along cobbled streets in the shadow of the Acropolis will find this favourite haunt, in which a giant copper still that once produced *raki* marks the way into the cool, dark interior of this unique setting. Along the wall are giant wooden barrels full of Vrettos's famous brandy, while bottles containing multi-coloured liqueurs like rose petal, citron, kumquat and cherry, not to mention the famous *mastiha* and *ouzo*, line the walls from floor to ceiling. Vrettos's marvellous atmosphere will immediately make you feel at home, and the die-hard regulars will welcome you as one their own.

20 Perivoli t'Ouranou

19 Lysikratous & 50 Leof Vassilissis Amalias

Regarded by many as the 'Greek blues', *rembetika* came from Asia Minor after the Catastrophe of 1922, when millions of refugees poured into Greece. They brought with them songs sung to the accompaniment of the traditional stringed *bouzouki*, telling of lost love, poverty, and the transitory nature of life. Perivoli t'Ouranou has a long history of *rembetika*, and stages performances by, among others, Babis Tsertos, considered by many to be the greatest *rembeti* singer today. When inspiration stirs the spirit, spontaneous performances break out to the mournful sounds of the *bouzouki*. For anyone wanting an intimate and authentic musical experience in Athens, Perivoli t'Ouranou, located directly across from Hadrian's Arch, is the place to go.

21 Dioscouri

13 Dioskouron

In Greek mythology, Castor and Pollux, the sons of Zeus, hatched out of eggs along with their sisters Helen of Troy and Clytemnestra and are known as the *dioskouri*. In addition to their roles as protectors of Athens, the twins were also associated with *theoxenia*, or a host-and-guest relationship with the gods, and as such were regarded as the patrons of hospitality. As one would expect, this café-*mezedopolio* makes every effort to live up to its illustrious name by serving *meze* in a distinguished environment. Located directly across from the Ancient Agora (see p. 54) overlooking the Temple of Hephaestus, Dioscouri is the ideal place for an afternoon *ouzo*. Order a *meze* platter for the table and share items like *tirokafteri* (spicy cheese dip) and *revithokroketes* (chickpea croquettes).

22 Ancient Agora

24 Adrianou

Once the centre of Athenian life, the Ancient Agora maintains its hold over the imagination with its remarkable ruins that span every period of Greece's past. One of the most delightful places to wander through is the grassy, tree-lined interior (carpeted with poppies in the spring), where even the most casual of strollers will happen upon the Temple of Hephaestus from classical antiquity, an 11th-century Byzantine church, and Hadrian's marble torso, a leftover from Roman occupation. While ambling through the Stoa of Attalos, it is easy to imagine Socrates holding forth amongst the market activity. Inside the Stoa is the tiny Agora Museum, which displays relics of Athens' nascent democracy, including *ostraka* (potsherds upon which were inscribed the names of tyrants to be ostracized), a *klepsydra* (a water-clock for timing speakers in the courts), and a *kleroterion* (a mechanism which randomly selected jurors in an attempt to avoid corruption).

OUT OF THE TOYBOX

23 To Kouti

23 Adrianou

This whimsical café-restaurant overlooking the Ancient Agora (see above) boasts an interior that looks as if a child were given free reign with the crayons. The quirky menus are handwritten in colourfully illustrated children's books, while toys, sand buckets and shovels are hung in a playful display to create a quaint, if somewhat eccentric, atmosphere. The name means 'the box', from the many peculiar old boxes in which chef-owner Eleni Kakoyianni's delicious home-made bread is served. Choices of dishes are unconventional, too, with a courgette soufflé and *formaella* cheese baked in vine leaves for starters, along with beef in garlic and honey and 'topless' shrimp with carrots, sesame and saffron, with a dash of cumin, for mains. Come in and play, for lunch or dinner.

ABYSSINIAN NIGHTS

24 Café Avyssinia

120

KEBABS A GO-GO
26 Thanasis
69 Mitropoleos

At any given moment day or night, Monastiraki is teeming with people going to and fro in a lively bazaar-like environment. At the centre of all this commotion is Thanasis, famous for its unrivalled shish kebab, made from marinated lamb and beef mince, formed on a skewer and grilled over an open fire. Order your kebab to go wrapped in a warm pita, slathered with *tzatzki* (yogurt and garlic sauce) and topped with fresh onions, or have a seat at a table on the sidewalk for the total experience, watching the crowds go by and listening to waiters call out orders. An obligatory part of the Monastiraki experience that is nutritious, delicious and inexpensive.

SOFRITO AND SKOPELITICO
27 Filistron
23 Apostolou Pavlou

While the food at Filistron is excellent, the main attraction here is definitely the view. From your table on the rooftop terrace you can gaze out to the Parthenon, hovering majestically over Athens and so it close it seems as if you could touch it. The dramatically lit Acropolis under a starry sky creates the perfect romantic atmosphere in which to enjoy a selection of Greek specialties. For starters, try one of the island pies such as the *cycladitico* (onion pie), or the twisted *skopelitico* with feta. Regional beef dishes like *sofrito* from Corfu, made with garlic and white wine, or beef *bardouniotiko* slow-cooked in a rich tomato and red wine sauce from Laconia are both recommended as main courses. The area around Filistron has many lively café-bars at which to complete a memorable evening out on the town.

CLOWNING AROUND
28 Edodi

DIAMONDS IN ORBIT
29 Ilias Lalaounis Jewelry Museum
12 Karyatidon & Kallisperi

This museum offers a glimpse into the history of jewelry-making through the designs of master goldsmith Ilias Lalaounis, with works that cover his career from 1940 to 2000. Located on the site of his father's workshop, where Lalaounis originally learned his craft, the permanent collection comprises over 3,000 pieces of jewelry and miniature sculptures, and includes works that are reminiscent of jewelry from the Minoan, Mycenaean and Byzantine eras, to pieces inspired by nature, including a 'DNA' series with its molecular motifs and the 'motion-in-space' series with its diamond-studded planets and golden orbits. The museum also organizes temporary exhibitions that include the applied and decorative arts. On the ground floor, visitors can experience the methods and materials of the goldsmith up close with a look into the studio, but beware of the gift shop – you may want one of everything.

INTIMATE BISTRO
30 Duende
2 Tziraion & 3 Dionisou Areopagitou

Still a well-kept secret, Duende is an intimate little bar with only ten tables and another ten bar stools. Its cool jazzy tunes, candlelight and antique mirrors make it a warm and cozy place for a glass of wine, served by the bottle or by the glass, from small local vineyards. Feeling a little like a French bistro, Duende offers cheese platters, avocado dip and a few light dishes-of-the-day, but is mainly a place for drinks. Family-run Duende is a favourite haunt of actors and artists, and attracts a more mature crowd. It is best to come early to get a seat as the place fills up after 11:00 p.m.

Omonia
Gazi
Psyrri

The downtown areas of Omonia, Votanikos, Gazi and Psyrri have received the most dramatic upgrades in recent years, with the 2004 Summer Olympics accelerating the completion of much-needed projects that seemed mired in perpetual construction. Omonia in particular saw the removal of the unsightly billboards that had infested the area and a thorough cleanup of its seedy underbelly. The public works have been a catalyst for a multicultural flourishing, and new businesses lining Sofokleous promise to inspire further development in the area. Progressive initiatives such as the Bacaro multispace (see. p. 122) and Fresh Hotel (see p. 88) are thriving. With Athens having the lowest crime rate in Europe, these downtrodden districts were not off-putting to tourists in the past for their violent reputations, but rather because they had no real draw, a situation that is rapidly changing thanks to all of this new development.

Psyrri was another neighbourhood that experienced an incredible renaissance, a claim which may seem dubious to newcomers to the area until they are miraculously transported from the derelict buildings and gritty side streets to the heart of one of the most vibrant areas in Athens. Psyrri is teeming with bohemian bars and clubs, and tavernas with live Greek music. It is swarming with people of all ages, all day, every day, and gypsies selling fragrant gardenias add to the festive atmosphere. Many designers have moved their ateliers here, attracted by the artsy atmosphere, while eccentric shops selling unique works of art or hand-made clothing have also cropped up. Unfortunately, as with all areas that find themselves suddenly at the centre of a new trend, quality has eroded somewhat at a few eateries, but there is always a good time, with much local colour and charm, to be had.

Nearby Gazi is a new up-and-coming area, with the Technopolis complex (see p. 69) as its centrepiece. A former gasworks factory, recently transformed into a magnificent new cultural centre, Technopolis hosts state-of-the-art exhibitions, musical performances, art events, and much more. Modern tavernas have emerged around this enlightened city project, alongside progressive Mediterranean mezedopolia that put a twist on tradition both in their flavours and in the décor. Barflies will love haunts overlooking Votanikos, with its ethereal towers silhouetted against the night sky. Votanikos is still in its early development stages, but already open is the Athinais multicomplex (see p. 69), offering a choice of restaurants, galleries, and concert halls, together with a cinema with a retractable roof.

1 Ideal

46 Panepistimiou

Return to La Belle Époque at Ideal, one of the oldest restaurants in Athens. A complete renovation in 1990 restored it to the splendour of its heyday in 1922, when it first opened its doors. Designs inspired by the sensuous opulence of the Art Déco period can be seen in the light fixtures, stained-glass ceilings and floral motifs on the walls. Everywhere you look, it is possible to appreciate the efforts that have gone into indulging the senses. The cuisine is classic Greek fare with some of the best *keftedakia* (meatballs) you are ever likely to encounter, made with *ouzo* and cumin, or try the braised lamb shank in a white wine sauce with oregano and feta cheese. Ideal's central location just off Omonia Square makes it a popular meeting place for those nostalgic for a bygone era.

CATCH OF THE DAY

2 Trata O Stelios

7 Themistokleous & 9 Nikitara

No one knows Stelios's real surname, for both he and his taverna go by the nickname given to him by long-time customers. The name 'Stelios-*trata*' comes from a special fishing net, a tribute to his reputation for having the freshest fish in the neighbourhood. Stelios's suppliers send him only the best seafood directly from his native Naxos, Aegina, and the southern coast of the Peloponnesus. One of the most popular dishes is *psarosoupa*, a soup made from many different varieties of fish and vegetables and blended into a rich and velvety purée. Other signature dishes include seafood pasta made with shrimp, langoustines, clams, *gialisteres*, and mussels, and spinach croquettes with diced squid and octopus, which you may find yourself describing on a postcard home.

GALLERY ANARCHY

3 Rebecca Camhi

80 Themistokleous, Plateia Exarchia

When Rebecca Camhi opened her gallery in the grittiest part of town in 1995, other galleries quickly followed suit and brought an artsy flavour and new life to what many considered to be the wrong side of the tracks. Having established a name for herself and her bold initiatives, she has recently relocated to Exarchia, once the bastion of anarchists and a no-go zone for the rest. The area has undergone a major cleanup and is now home to many cafés and bars, while retaining its underground atmosphere. Camhi's light-filled gallery is located in a Bauhaus building off Exarchia's main square, and exhibitions feature such artists as Nan Goldin, Karen Kilimnik, Miltos Manetas, Nobuyoshi Araki, Ross Bleckner, DeAnna Maganias and Julian Opie.

VENETIAN PLEASURE

4 Bacaro

122

BRAVO FOR COFFEE

5 Mokka

44 Athinas

Unravelling the history of Mokka takes one back to 1922, when Nikos Psomas's family founded the Bravo company, celebrated for its fine-ground Greek coffee. Three generations later, coffee is still in the blood of this youthful entrepreneur, who oversees all aspects of the business and buys direct from producers all over the world, from Brazil to Ethiopia, to ensure the best quality. Located beside Athens' largest outdoor market, the Varvakios Agora (see p. 65) on the hectic fringe of Athinas, Mokka continues the legacy of a product that has changed the social fabric of Greek society. Here, you have the added luxury of having your coffee freshly ground and roasted on the premises by a barista whose knowledge is evident from the first sip.

SUMPTUOUS MUSEUM

6 Benaki Museum of Islamic Art

22 Agion Asomaton & 12 Dipylou

The Benaki Museum's (see p. 40) new annexe houses Antonis Benaki's collection of Islamic art, spanning the 7th to the 19th centuries. The museum holds over 10,000 objects, of which about 1,500 are displayed at any one time. The Islamic love of sumptuous materials and rich decoration is apparent in the collection's elaborately patterned ceramics, intricate metalwork, ornate woodcarvings, delicate glassware, textiles, gold jewelry, tombstones, illuminated manuscripts, astronomical instruments, arms and armour, an even a lavish marble floor from a 17th-century mansion in Cairo. Located in the Keramikos district in a neoclassical house donated by Lambros Eftaxias, the exhibits are organized chronologically over four floors, and include works from Babylonia to Egypt. The Benaki is one of the most significant collections of Islamic art in Europe, and offers an insightful journey through the fascinating culture of the Muslim world.

7 Fresh Hotel
FRESH AND INVITING

8 Elixir
HERBAL REMEDIES

41 Evripidou

At Elixir you will find a spectacular array of herbs and spices displayed in antique wood-and-glass cabinets. Beneath dried fruits and vegetables hanging from the ceiling are tables stacked with lavender, cinnamon sticks, vanilla pods, and the famous Kozani saffron, along with different varieties of local honey, from chestnut and pine, to thyme and orange blossom. There are also shelves of olive oil soaps along with frankincense and myrrh to scent and purify your home, and, some believe, rid it of evil spirits. Many Greeks swear by the therapeutic tea and wild mountain herbs sourced from all over the country as homeopathic remedies.

9 Krinos
DONUT INDULGENCE

87 Aiolou

No one who happens to be out for a stroll down Aiolou can resist stopping in at Krinos for their famous *loukoumades*. This is not the place to be calorie conscious, so go ahead and surrender to the charms of the Greek version of a donut, deep-fried to order and then drenched in hot honey syrup and finished off with a sprinkle of cinnamon. Alternatively, try the *bougatsa*, a flakey phyllo pastry pie filled with decadent custard cream, baked in the oven and served warm with a drizzle of honey and dash of cinnamon. Krinos's appeal knows no age limits and is loved by young and old alike at any hour of the day – from breakfast to after dinner. Dieting begins tomorrow.

10 Varvakios Agora
TO MARKET, TO MARKET

Athinas, between Sofokleous and Evripidou

Athens' largest open-air market, the Varvakios (municipal) market, is located on Athinas, connecting Monastiraki with Omonia, and attracts shoppers with both the enormous variety of foodstuffs on offer as well as the low prices. It's an experience in itself just to stroll amongst the colourful displays of cheese, seasonal produce, barrels of olives, hanging sausages, and fish of every variety, with vendors loudly extolling the virtues of their wares to entice customers towards their stalls. Behind Varvakios Agora is the meat market, with whole lambs and chickens hung over trays overflowing with offal, sweetbreads and liver, a veritable carnivore's dream and reminiscent of a Dutch still-life painting. Just along the way, Vorrias caters to all your dried fruit, seed and nut needs, while the appetite you work up taking it all in leads to the obligatory market dining experience at Diporto across the street (see below).

11 Diporto
DOOR-TO-DOOR

9 Sofokleous & Theatrou

Diporto, or 'two doors', is so named because this basement eatery has entrances on Theatrou and Sokratous (making it ideal for the lawless). Nothing has changed for over 50 years, from the giant barrels of *retsina* (a pine resin-flavoured wine) that take up half the taverna's interior space, to the hearty servings of chickpea soup or black-eyed beans that accompany grilled sardines or *barbounakia* red mullet, and boiled wild greens supplied from the Varvakios Agora (see above) across the street. Whatever Barba Mitsos is cooking is what you are having in this wonderfully authentic, no-frills tavern. You will know you have come to the right place when you see vendors from the market eating at tables beside you.

12 Arhaion Gefsis
HAPPY EATING

22 Kodratou

The hedonistic doctrine of the Epicurean school maintained that securing a happy life was all-important, and that happiness had pleasure as its beginning and end. In the ancient literature on pleasure, including Archistratus' *The Life of Luxury* and Heracleides' *Art of Cookery*, we have a glimpse of the pleasures of the cuisine from which Arhaion Gefsis ('ancient flavours') draws its inspiration. Amidst flaming torches and classical columns, you will be served dishes based on ancient recipes by *chiton*-wearing servers in a setting reminiscent of Plato's Symposium. Overlooking the decidedly kitsch atmosphere is easier once the honeyed wine begins to flow. Savour dishes such as garlicky chickpea purée and pork with prunes and thyme, eaten with a spoon and knife (and no fork) as the ancients once did.

13 Telis
86 Evripidou, Koumoundourou Square

Although located in a less than picturesque part of town, Telis is set at the heart of the city's multicultural area. Those who have forgotten their maps can follow the smell of grilled pork or the sound of clarinets and accordions wafting down Evripidou. The *Epirotika* songs from northern Greece might even inspire a reveller to an impromptu streetside dance. In the centre of all this merriment, unruffled by it all, is Mr Telis himself, who for nearly 30 years has presided over mounds of *brizoles* (pork chops) sizzling away on the grill, which are always served with fried potatoes. It is a lively atmosphere in which spirits run high and prices are low.

GOOD TIMES IN GAZI
14 Mamacas
41 Persophones

Mamacas embraces the seeming contradiction of old-fashioned home cooking in a modern, lively environment. Along with the traditional taverna-style menu, also on offer is superlative people-watching, as the restaurant has become the favoured haunt of actors and models attracted to an unpretentious scene that still manages to have a bit of attitude. Whitewashed wooden floorboards and ceiling beams warm up the all-cream atmosphere, creating an airy and vibrant setting that is always overflowing with diners. Mamacas was among the first to settle in this rundown part of Gazi, which is rapidly transforming into a colourful and happening multi-ethnic district.

IN A YELLOW BICYCLE
15 Kitrino Podilato
116 Keramikou & Iera Odos

The name of the café means 'yellow bicycle', and chef Nikos Pouliassis's creative, Greek-with-a-twist cuisine is certainly worth cycling any distance to experience. Begin with an unconventional version of *trahana* soup, milk-drenched bulgur wheat that is sun-dried and then simmered with tomatoes and served with feta cheese mousse, or try the unusual risotto with beetroot and anchovy pesto. For dessert, forget everything you know about tiramisu and try Pouliassis's version, made with white aubergines from Santorini and topped with a drizzle of rosemary oil! The intimate, candlelit interior and the memorable dishes persuade you to leave that bicycle parked outside just a little longer.

Mamacas

16 Athinais

34-36 Kastorias

This converted silk factory in the rundown neighbourhood of Votanikos has been transformed into a multipurpose complex that hosts conferences and art exhibitions, both ancient and modern. It also features a theatre, concert hall and open-air cinema showing film classics. Hungry? The excellent restaurant Red is located here, too, as well as the more casual brasserie Votanikos and Boiler Bar. Originally designed by Thomas Gazetas in the 1920s, the recent renovation, completed in 2000, was overseen by husband-and-wife team Nassos Kokkineas and Marilena Mamidakis. The 6,500-square-metre building's exposed stone, glass and steel elements have been retained to preserve its original industrial style, and to provide an impressive forum for culture, business and entertainment under one roof.

LEFT AND RIGHT

17 Aristera Dexia

106

FACTORY TURNED MUSEUM

18 Benaki Museum Pireos Annexe

138 Pireos & Andronikou

This new museum hosts high-profile exhibitions and cultural events in a recently renovated 1960s industrial building. The museum was inaugurated along with the Benaki Museum of Islamic Art (see p. 62) by director Antonis Delivorias just in time for the 2004 Summer Olympics. Following the trend for factory-to-art-centre renovations, architects Maria Kokkinou and Andreas Kourkoulas have responded to contemporary needs with yet another successful conversion. The building, clad in a handsome dusky-plum marble, covers an entire block of Pireos and contains a vast atrium lined with movable blinds and steel mesh, a 400-seat amphitheatre, a bookstore and architectural archive, as well as a stylish café.

DRINKS AT THE GASWORKS

19 Gazarte

32-34 Voutadon

Gazarte sets the scene with its view overlooking the recently renovated gasworks factory that has become Technopolis (see below). Gazarte is a multi-use complex with a cinema and live-performance space downstairs that also stages art exhibitions, and a lounge-bar and restaurant upstairs. In warm weather, dine outside in sight of Technopolis on the open terrace. The neon red glow of the smokestacks pierces the night sky and creates a magical setting in which to enjoy a dinner of Mediterranean cuisine and late-night dancing.

GLAMOROUS BOUZOUKIA

20 Athens Arena

CULTURAL COMPLEX

21 Technopolis

100 Pireos

The former gasworks factory, from which the Gazi area takes its name, has been transformed into Technopolis, or 'city of the arts', an extraordinary multipurpose cultural centre in what was once one of the most rundown parts of the city. Many of the factory's boiler rooms and pumping stations have been preserved, with pieces of the original machinery intact. After renovation, they now host art exhibitions, happenings, festivals and concerts. The city's main radio station is also located here, as is as a museum dedicated to Greece's beloved opera diva, Maria Callas.

A JOURNEY OF FLAVOUR

22 Prosopa

84 Konstantinoupoleos

The romance of rail travel lends to the atmosphere of this genial little restaurant beside the train tracks on the outskirts of the Gazi district. Old gas factories once dominated the area, but many see the neighbourhood as the next up-and-coming part of the city. Just when wanderlust is about to set in with the passing of another train, fine flavours arrive interrupting your imaginary travels to destinations unseen. On the menu are the scents and tastes of the Mediterranean, including a wide array of pasta and risotto entrées, as well as a few beef, chicken, pork and seafood dishes. The proprietors are young and enthusiastic, and attract a growing following with their hospitality and gracious yet relaxed service.

23 Varoulko

115

24 Rakoselektes

25 Aisopou & Karaiskaki

The name means 'raki connoisseurs', indicating this is the place to get to know Greece's 'firewater'. *Raki* (also called *tsikoudia* or *tsipouro*) is a traditional distilled spirit drunk in small glasses and accompanied by a continuous flow of small plates of *meze*. Occupying two levels with monastery-style tables, wooden chairs and exposed masonry, Rakoselektes's rustic and relaxed setting is conducive to drinking liberal amounts of its soul-warming namesake in the company of friends. A popular accompaniment is exquisite *avgotaraho*, fish roe (or *bottarga*) from Missolonghi sealed in protective wax. Or try a village favourite, *kayiana*, made from scrambled eggs with feta cheese, tomatoes and onions, and occasionally sautéed courgettes and potatoes for a heartier version.

MUSSELS AND MEZE

25 Baxevani Saffron

Psyrri

One of Athens' most talked about new chefs is Yiannis Baxevanis, who recently made his name with the restaurant Hytra. He has given his name to this new venture, located in a beautifully restored neoclassical building in the lively Psyrri area. The dining experience begins upon arrival when you are welcomed with several small *meze* dishes, which depend on what the chef found fresh that day in the market. For mains, choose from mussels and rice with *glistrida* or the more pungent flavour of salted cod served in a mild garlic sauce with nettles. The comfortable interior is classic yet modern, spacious yet intimate, and is an ideal setting in which to savour an evening of aromas and flavours to which your mind will return when you plan a repeat visit to this rising star.

SHOES LIKE POETRY

26 Melissinos

2 Agia Theklasi

Sandal-maker and self-styled poet Stavros Melissinos has been making hand-made leather sandals for over 50 years. His classically inspired designs are custom-fitted for his customers, who have in the past included all four Beatles, Jackie Onassis and Sophia Loren. Scattered amidst the tools of his trade are clippings from the countless articles that have been written about Melissinos. Part of the experience of getting fitted for a pair of his celebrated shoes is being made privy to his poetry recitations. The clutter and poetry may prompt you to share a Zen-inspired thought by Lin-Chi: 'When you meet a master swordsman, show him your sword. When you meet a man who is not a poet, do not show him your poem.'

ELEGANCE IN SIMPLICITY

27 Vasso Consola

1-3 Sahtouri & Sari

Vasso Consola's elegant fashion designs, many of which are inspired by the diaphanous simplicity of the garments of ancient Greece, evoke the word 'architecture' as she creates an environment in which the body can move freely, beautifully expressing the individuality of the wearer. Other pieces are reminiscent of the 1920s, and create a sense of nostalgia while dispelling any idea of homogeneity of style. Whether they are loose-fitting silks or more revealing stretchy knitwear the philosophy is similar; a seamless flow favouring geometric cuts. Consola's subdued colours and subtle play of textures result in a complete look from which jewelry and other accessories would only detract.

FASHION'S FAVOURITE

28 Yiorgos Eleftheriades

134

Glyfada
Vouliagmeni
Voula
Piraeus

As it was in classical times, Piraeus is still the main port of Athens and is one of the busiest ports in the world. Although today most visitors venture down to Piraeus only to catch a ferry to the islands (see pp. 150–69), it is a colourful place to explore in its own right. Piraeus is linked to Athens by Syngrou and Pireos Avenues, or by a 20-minute train ride. These routes still follow the 'long walls', parts of which are still visible today, built by Themistocles in 480 BC to protect Athens from the Persian invasion. The most popular place to while away an afternoon sampling fresh seafood is the well-trodden Mikrolimano ('little port'), or head to Zea Marina for a coffee or cocktail at sunset while looking out to sea. Both are picturesque harbours lined with bars, restaurants and cafés with a club scene that comes alive at night.

Piraeus is full of character and steeped in history (be sure to visit the Archaeological Museum of Piraeus and the Hellenic Maritime Museum), and immortalized in the film *Never on Sunday*. The lovely neoclassical buildings provide a stark contrast to the quaint neighbourhoods of humble single-storey houses, the legacy of refugees who flooded into Greece after the Catastrophe of 1922 and brought with them the soulful sounds of *rembetika*, once illegal but which has since been embraced as classic. A trek through the pretty neighbourhood of Castella is also worthwhile, as is continuing up to Profiti Ilias for magnificent views over the Gulf to Aegina (see p. 150). Down in the lively central market, visit the fish stalls and soak up the atmosphere of the backstreets and the many eccentric specialty shops.

The coastal Leof Posidonos takes you to what locals have dubbed the 'Athenian Riviera', Glyfada and Vouliagmeni, a playground for Athenians in the summer when winter businesses close up shop, and luxurious open-air nightclubs, bars and restaurants open along the seafront. Every year these trendy venues change décor and attract the beautiful people, who come scantily clad and gorgeously bronzed to party till sunrise. During the day there are many beaches to choose from, some offering (for a fee) lounge chairs, umbrellas, changing rooms, and other amenities. Should you desire something more secluded, visit one of the sandy coves or rocky shores where it is possible to find complete solitude, even at the peak of the summer season. Nearby you can take a therapeutic soak in Lake Vouliagmeni (see p. 79), or luxuriate in the resort atmosphere of Kavouri. The commercial centre of Glyfada offers excellent shopping with top-name designer shops lining every street, along with upmarket café-bars and restaurants, as well as the nearby Glyfada Golf Club (see p. 76) for a few rounds before being spoiled for choice for the evening's entertainment.

1 Skipper's Yacht 'n' Roll

Pier 1, Alimos Marina

This café-by-the-sea is the haunt of choice for aspiring pirates with its beautiful galleon moored alongside, inspiring many a fantasy of buried treasure and adventure on the high seas. Located down by Pier 1 between a boatyard and the harbour, this atmospheric café-bar looks out onto hundreds of sailboats and yachts in Alimos, the largest marina in the country. You will find no high design, fancy cocktails, or bejeweled divas here. This unpretentious venue is as authentic as it gets with people of all backgrounds, from hired deckhands to business magnates, college students to pensioners, all sitting shoulder-to-shoulder out on the wooden deck enjoying life's simple pleasures.

BEACH BUNNIES

2 Akrotiri

5 Vasileos Georgiou B

This massive beachside dance club continually draws a capacity crowd of up to 3,000 partygoers, mostly 20- to 30-somethings who dance the night away amidst swathes of gauzy white curtains fluttering in the sea breeze. Akrotiri's island-inspired setting has a distinctly tropical feel, with a background of R&B, pop, and the occasional Greek chart hit. Prepare for a long night of revelling in this lush and happening venue. At daybreak, there is usually a group of diehards who end up on the shore to watch a glorious magenta-coloured sunrise and to indulge in a rejuvenating dip at Agios Kosmas beach as the party winds down at last.

TAKE A SWING

3 Glyfada Golf Club

Terma Pronois

It may not be the Royal & Ancient Golf Club of St Andrews, but this course offers avid golfers the opportunity to indulge their passion only 8 kilometres from central Athens, and an hour from the airport. Although golf is still in its nascent stages in Greece, it is rapidly growing in popularity. Located in the southern seaside suburb of Glyfada, the club was founded in 1962 and and boasts fairways stretching across 650 acres. It is an 18-hole, par 72 course with about 1,000 permanent members. Due to Greece's moderate climate, the club is open all year round, and sports a pro shop catering to all your golfing needs. Who said golf is a good walk spoilt?

STARS IN THEIR EYES

4 O Serkos & Tesera Asteria

114

REGIONAL BEST

5 To Bakaliko Ola Ta Kala

1 Artemidos, Esperidon Square

The name means 'a deli with all the best', and with good reason. Bakaliko is a delicatessen offering only the finest products sourced from small suppliers from all over Greece. Here you will discover over 20 brands of the purest virgin olive oil, olives from around the country, hand-made pasta, fava beans from Santorini, mouthwatering sweets (including *loukoumia*, or 'Greek delight', from Syros), thyme-scented honey from Kythira, goat's cheese from Naxos, and much more. Alongside these classics are such unusual items as pomegranate marmalade and candied courgettes, together with traditional spirits. Can't decide? Then stay for lunch and sample the many specialties of the house, including puréed fava beans with marinated caper leaves, feta in sesame seeds, and pork with figs and caramelized apples. 'All the best', indeed.

DESIGNER CAFÉ

6 Café Café

122

POTTERY, PLEASE

7 Ionia

23 Grigoriou Lambraki

With the factory on the island of Evia and its offices in Athens, Ionia turns out high-quality, durable porcelain created by top designers in the field. Many of the patterns are inspired by the national landscape, and incorporate characteristically Greek motifs and colours. Marine themes with fish, sailboats and waves, along with olives and grapevines, appear in designs that range from bold and colourful with splashes of sunshine yellow and ocean blue, to more subtly textured patterns. Whether you are looking for a complete dinner set or a souvenir of your travels, Ionia has innovative designs that are certain to provide pleasure at your table for many years to come.

SHOES FOR ALL OCCASIONS

8 Danos

61 Kyprou

For 30 years the Danos label has been sought after by discerning Athenian women as a mark of quality designer footwear. Originally a small company making exclusively hand-made shoes, demand during the 1980s prompted the brand to expand and incorporate the latest technology into the manufacturing process. Today the quality associated with the name continues with the present team of designers who create styles to suit women of all ages and use the best materials available to make comfortable, fashionable shoes for both formal and casual occasions. Stores in Kolonaki, Kifissia and this one in Glyfada also carry international brands like Donna Karan, Pucci, and Mario Cerutti, which are available alongside the Danos collection.

SOMETHING FISHY

9 Lambros

20 Leof Posidonos

All thoughts of diving into the clear blue water below disappear as soon as Mr Lambros starts serving up his classic seafood dishes in this charming Greek taverna. Perched above a quiet cove directly across from Lake Vouliagmeni, Lambros has had a loyal following since opening in 1939. The secret to surviving the test of time is ensuring that your customers know they will find only the freshest seafood available, and that it will be prepared to perfection. This is Lambros's promise and they deliver. Come to experience such traditional favourites as grilled octopus, poached sole, or the wonderfully flavourful pan-fried red mullet. Or try a fish unique to the Aegean, such as *melanouria, mourmoures, katsoules,* or whatever else is fresh from the sea that day.

10 Pere Ubu

74 Kyprou

Owner Spyros Kombitsis brought together an eclectic mix of over a dozen designers with a predilection for the minimal, unique and appealing to create this Glyfada restaurant. Names such as Ingo Maurer, Stagedesignoffice, Knoll, B&B Italia and Flos are a few of the designers whose aesthetics have contributed to the artsy look of this contemporary space. Chef Kostas Tsigas's creative menu is well suited to a tasting trip through the wine list of over 30 labels, available by the glass to accompany dishes like artichoke and smoked fish roe, duck breast with date chutney, and a divine cheese soufflé. Diners will leave this cross between a modern wine bar and traditional brasserie knowing that they have had a fine meal – deliciously prepared, beautifully presented, and reasonably priced.

11 Lake Vouliagmeni & Health Spa

Leof Posidonos

This dramatic rocky setting with its mystical aura has been a place of healing since ancient times. Formerly an underground cavern that collapsed during an earthquake (the name means 'sunken lake'), Lake Vouliagmeni is perpetually replenished from mineral-rich hot springs 100 metres below sea level. The water is believed to have therapeutic qualities beneficial for treating a host of ailments, particularly arthritis and skin disorders. There is also a well-run café that serves fruit drinks, coffee and snacks directly to you as you relax in the sun and enjoy the beautiful surroundings. The lake remains a comfortable 21–27°C year-round, offering visitors the opportunity to 'take the waters' in any season, restoring both mind and body in this natural spa only 30 minutes from Athens.

DANCE BY THE SEASIDE
12 Balux

FRANCOPHILE
13 Septum

A DAY ON THE WATER
14 Lolos Ski Centre
Vouliagmeni Yacht Club

Whether you are a professional waterskier or a total beginner, you will find all you need to kit yourself out for a run on the water at Lolos Ski Centre. For owner Stamatis Lolos skiing is more than a hobby or a job, it is a way of life. This passion is reflected at the centre, from the professional equipment to the expert lessons. The ski club is located inside the Vouliagmeni Yacht Club, just down the road from Astir beach. The setting is glamorous, the waters pristine, and the attendants worthy of adorning the Parthenon frieze. Open year-round until sunset, the centre also offers facilities for other watersports, including surfing and inner-tubing.

LUXURIOUS RESORT
15 Astir Palace Resort

TRANQUIL BAR
16 Zen
Vouliagmenis Marina

Known to locals as 'the Moorings' for the small yachting marina that it overlooks, the Zen-inspired aesthetics of this waterfront bar exclude anything that would obstruct your gaze out over the Saronic Gulf. Subdued amber lighting, pale wooden floors, wicker chaise longues, and the sound of the waves below combine to make this a favourite summertime gathering place. In winter, the folding glass walls are reassembled, creating the impression that the bar is still open to the sun and sea. Spend a leisurely afternoon lounging with a cocktail, or arrive later to enjoy the romantic atmosphere of the marina by night. Just a few minutes walk from Astir Palace Resort (see p. 100), this is a lovely spot to come to for a quiet drink – quiet, that is, until the partying begins after midnight.

SIPPING BY THE POOL
20 Pisina
25 Akti Themistokleous, Zea Marina

Named after the swimming pool around which the café-bar is arranged, Pisina is located in the picturesque Zea Marina with its profusion of luxury yachts. In the distance is Castella, the most attractive area of Piraeus, with its towering mosaic of villas and apartments clinging to the hillside in the manner of a Cubist painting. All kinds of coffees are served – from the super-caffeinated frappe to the ever-popular freddo – brought to you poolside by waiters appropriately attired in turquoise blue and seaweed green. A canopied section is reserved for dining poolside in the shade, while sofas and space-age chrome lighting fixtures inspire extended stays. And if it gets too hot, you can always cool down with a dip in the pool.

THE LION'S SHARE
21 To Liondari Tou Piraeus
20 Marias Xatzikiriakou

After defeating the Turks in 1684, Venice claimed as a trophy the famous lion statue that gave the harbour its name, 'Porto Leone'. That lion still stands guard over the Venetian Arsenal today. In its place, a modern sculpture by George Megoulas watches over this charming seaside square and the café with its commanding views over the bustling port. All manner of ships cruise in and out to the sound of the old clock tower chiming the hour with the familiar theme from *Never on Sunday*, which was filmed in Piraeus. The Lion's enchanting atmosphere is ideal for an afternoon *ouzo*, accompanied by a mixed *meze* platter or coffee served with Mrs Tasia's delectable *loukoumades*, home-made donuts drenched in warm honey with a sprinkle of cinnamon – the best you'll find anywhere.

22 Café Waichhart
58 Akti Moutsopoulou

A visit to Café Waichhart is a nostalgic trip back in time. The atmosphere is redolent of 1930s Vienna, complete with Thonet bentwood chairs and a bar made from a hand-carved mahogany pharmacy from Lesvos and pieces of an old luxury liner. Lining the walls, amidst gilt mirrors and wooden cabinets containing vintage Champagne bottles, are portraits of beautiful women and a photo of a young orphan, inscribed with the sitter's wish that it be hung at a gathering place of friends to ensure that he would never be lonely again. Choose from the many rice and pasta dishes, and enjoy the romantic atmosphere of a bygone era.

NAUTICAL NOSH
23 Jimmy & the Fish

114

SEAFOOD MEZE
24 Kollias
3 Stratigou Plastira

Tucked away in the backstreets of a rundown neighbourhood of Piraeus is this gem of a restaurant. No longer a well-kept secret, Kollias has gained a cult following of *opsofagi*, or 'fish lovers', who are passionately devoted to the place. The demitasse of fish soup served upon arrival is a prelude to the memorable meal that is about to begin. Ordering begins in the kitchen, where you choose from an array of dishes from mushrooms stuffed with shrimp, pasta and cuttlefish baked in its own ink, to live clams, sea urchins and mussels. The best course of action is to order a variety of small plates and share.

SPICE WORLD
25 Mandragoras
14 Gounaris

Mandragoras is just the sort of old-fashioned shop you would expect to find in Greece's largest port, packed full with aromas and colours evocative of the days when ships arrived with exotic treasures from the silk and spice routes. Divided into two shops with a 1920s décor, Mandragoras has wall-to-wall shelves piled high with herbs, tea, essential oils, incense and soap, and drawers full of spices, seeds and roots. Next door are barrels of olives and sacks of pulses, salt-cured fish, braids of garlic and fiery peppers, wheels of cheese, traditional sweets and a selection of wine. A fascinating visit sure to entice all the senses.

sleep

A few years ago designer boutique hotels were practically unknown in Athens, but service-industry standards have improved dramatically in the post-Olympics era. New hotels, including Semiramis, Periscope and Twenty One (all part of art collector Dakis Joannou's empire), emphasize the integration of art and design. Today they offer not only stunning views and rooftop pools, but also luxurious, ultra-modern facilities that have sparked a revolution among the city's stylish places to sleep. From the southern seaside suburb of Kavouri to the breezy pine-clad oasis of Ekali in the north, a new spirit of luxury is in the warm Athenian air.

Sofokleous Street is also home to the Athens Stock Exchange and offers a bustling, if unusual, mix of suited-and-booted city workers and immigrant merchants plying their wares. In the midst of this lively scene, like a breath of fresh air, is the radically renovated and appropriately named Fresh Hotel.

Architects Tassos Zeppos and Eleni Georgiadi at AIRTEC used vivid colours and unconventional design to create a relaxed, informal setting for this stylish urban retreat. The reception area, separated from the rest of the hotel by fuchsia glass, is set off by a dramatically vertical black fireplace, illuminated from above by an imposing lighting fixture by Martinelliluce, resembling an unfurling white lotus, and leather sofas by Morosa that appear to have been poured into the foyer. Venturing up the marble staircase, also black, to the mezzanine leads weary travellers to the gym, sauna, and steam room, along with business centres that are transparent, yet completely private. The hotel's 133 rooms offer all the peaceful solace of a Japanese garden, particularly the balconies which are strewn with grey-and-white sea pebbles and planters filled with exotic foliage. One suite has a curvaceous bath in the bedroom, which is both a functional and aesthetic feature of the room.

A good place to start the day is the Magenta Restaurant, offering a menu with lots of choices for the health conscious and located next to the conference rooms. On the ninth floor the Air Lounge Bar, with its wooden deck and swimming pool, affords lovely views of the Acropolis and serves cocktails, fresh fruit drinks, and snacks. The hotel's main eatery is the Orange Bar Restaurant, which overlooks the street and serves customers all day and well into the night. Its menu of light meals relies on fresh ingredients from the neighbouring Varvakios Agora (see p. 65), Athens' central market. Splashes of pumpkin orange against the warm, walnut-brown floors create a feel-good atmosphere which you can snuggle into while sampling the over 30 wine labels offered by the glass.

44 Hotel Grande Bretagne

3 Syntagma Square
Rooms from €270

Originally built in 1842 as a private residence, this legendary landmark is a hotel of unrivalled opulence and is steeped in the city's history. Having recently undergone a lavish renovation project that cost over €70 million and took two years to complete, the hotel has been restored it to its former glory and the hand-carved architectural details, glittering gold-leaf meander motif, elegant ionic columns and fine antiques evoke its original 19th-century grandeur. Centrally located on Syntagma Square, the Hotel Grand Bretagne has seen the world's most famous personalities walk through its doors.

The 321 rooms and suites combine opulence with sophisticated technology, a happy marriage most clearly seen in the Royal and Presidential suites (400 and 160 generous square metres respectively), both of which surpass all previous notions of luxury. A private steam room, gym, fireplace, dining room, and a even wine cellar are among the amenities of these indulgent suites. Some of the standard rooms have small balconies and are not as spacious, but boast the same luxurious décor and mod cons. Wander into the winter garden with its lofty stained-glass ceiling, palm trees, and winged bronze statues for a suitably decadent atmosphere in which to have brunch or a very British afternoon tea, or quaff a cocktail in the Alexander Bar, named for the hand-made 18th-century tapestry depicting Alexander the Great on one of his exploits. Here you can pair a Grand Reserve cognac or vintage port with a cigar from the walk-in humidor.

Diners can opt for one (or more) of four venues: the brasserie-style GB Corner with its Mediterranean cuisine, a favourite haunt of ministers and high-profile businessmen; the roof garden, offering similar fare along with breathtaking views of the Parthenon; the exclusive dining space in the Churchill Room (named after the man himself who stayed here on several occasions); or a monastery table in the Cellar, amidst the 2,600 bottles that make up the hotel's wine collection. Afterwards, guests can take a plunge in the pool or relax in one of the city's best spas, because too much of everything is just enough...

HOTEL ON THE HILL

28 **St George Lycabettus**

1 2 Kleomenous
Rooms from €170

The recently redesigned and completely refurbished St George Lycabettus is situated high upon the slopes of Mt Lycabettus in the centre of Athens' most cosmopolitan area, Kolonaki. The main draw here is definitely the hotel's location, with sublime views of the city crowned by the Acropolis on one side and the tiny church of St George, from whence the hotel took its name, perched precariously above on the summit. Eccentric and eclectic, each floor, corridor and room is decorated with a different theme and styled accordingly with works by various Greek artists. Some have a 19th-century neoclassical atmosphere, while others are ultra-modern. The top-floor Presidential suite sports the uniquely Louis XIV-goes-to-Africa décor, with its animal-print lampshades and fur pillows, and boasts 100 square metres of balcony. The hotel has something to suit everyone's taste, but you may wish to opt for the corner rooms as they enjoy panoramic views with windows on two sides.

The location, nestled among the pine trees high above the city, ensures a constant breezy atmosphere, which is especially magical at night when the Parthenon is beautifully illuminated and appears to be floating dreamlike in the sky. To take full advantage of the hotel's setting, take in the view with a dip in the rooftop pool, enjoy a cocktail in the Sky Bar, or dine in Le Grand Balcon restaurant, which serves up nouvelle Greek cuisine in an eccentrically decorated interior designed by Angelos Angelopoulos. Tree-trunk cocktail tables, strings of crystal beads cascading from the bar, and silver leather sofas set off with a splattering of fuchsia taffeta make for an intriguing atmosphere that has been called everything from 'rock baroque' to 'Alice-steps-through-the-looking-glass-and-ends-up-in-Las Vegas'. Another place in which to lose oneself is the spa, with its undulating lavender walls permeated with the scent of essential oils. For a more down-to-earth experience, there is the casual restaurant-bar, Frame (see p. 128), with its 1970s-revival décor.

ART SMART
 Twenty One
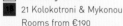
21 Kolokotroni & Mykonou
Rooms from €190

It is not surprising to find that 'art' is a persistent theme in Dakis Joannou's hotels. After all, he owns one of the largest and most important modern art collections in Greece. Luckily for Athens and her visitors, he has chosen to share the wealth of his creative vision by commissioning several hotels, including Semiramis (see p. 98), Periscope (see p. 102), and Twenty One (along with the Deste Foundation; see p. 17), in which art transcends museum boundaries to play a more than merely decorative role.

Running through each of Twenty One's 21 rooms is a unified work by local Greek artist, Georgia Sagri, that can be viewed as a whole in the (miniature) copy on display in the reception area, or appreciated separately in each guestroom, in which a different section of Sagri's work is featured on one of its walls. The painting, reminiscent of a child set free with a box of crayons – albeit with slightly more sinister undertones – is in stark contrast with the clean, definitive lines of the super-sleek red, white and charcoal-grey interior. The furniture, cleverly fitted into the architecture, rolls out over wooden floors from what appears to be a seamless puzzle. The combined elements are bathed in light, resulting in a youthful energy that permeates the space. Of the rooms, five are loft suites with two levels connected by internal stairs and skylights positioned over the fluffy, cloud-like beds.

The café-bar and restaurant serve excellent cocktails and modern Mediterranean cuisine, and provide an informal setting for drinking, dining, and relaxing at all hours of the day.

BUSINESS AND PLEASURE
14 **Life Gallery Athens**
2F 103 Thiseos
Rooms from €250

The Mamidakis group's high-design concept for Life Gallery Athens creates a welcome respite with a refined sense of balance. Located in the residential area of Ekali, an hour from the city centre and 15 minutes from Kifissia's commercial district, this intimate property set amongst the cedars and pine trees was designed for leisure and pleasure, with a perfect balance between architecture and nature, and one's place in it. Architects Klein/Haller and Vassilis Rodatos created this minimalist sanctuary with its subtle variety of earth tones, natural textures and airy spaciousness that give this small luxury hotel the feeling of a secluded retreat.

Life Gallery's 30 rooms include three suites, three art studios and 24 open-plan deluxe rooms, all of which have ample seating areas, verandas with uninterrupted views, and sensual lighting. The living space incorporates cleverly designed bathrooms stocked with Korres products (see p. 49), and extends to encompass a functional work space. Works by such contemporary Greek artists as Takis, Kessanlis, Lappas and Gyparakis adorn the walls, while drinks and ethnic music flow in the Pisco Sour bar. All of the furniture has been created by top international designers, including Gervasoni, Molteni and Interni. In the summer, the expansive bar spills out into the pool area, where diners can enjoy drinks and dinner al fresco in a cool, relaxing atmosphere, complete with comfortable wicker chairs at the poolside restaurant Avenue 103. Overlooking the pool is a wonderful library where you can submerge yourself in both the cozy armchairs and in the fine collection of books devoted to Greek literature, art and history.

Also at the Life Gallery is the obligatory spa, complete with every indulgent feature you could ask for, including a meditation room filled with flickering aromatic tea lights. It seems almost sacrilegious to mention the conference centre in a place so disposed to relaxation, but the facilities make for the ideal setting in which to combine business with pleasure.

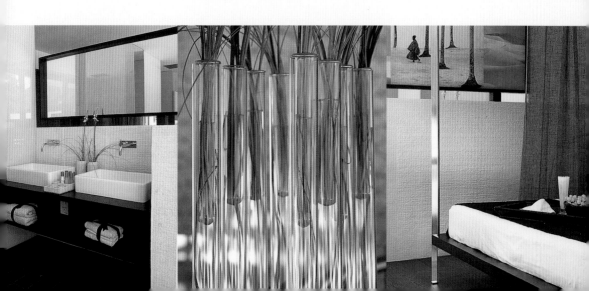

When Dakis Joannou commissioned internationally acclaimed designer Karim Rashid to create Greece's first 'design' hotel, the inevitable result was something unique and dynamic. Located in the quiet northern suburb of Kifissia in shady Kefalari Square, the hotel strives to create an ultra-modern oasis informed by cool and contemporary design.

Rashid's innovative design combines functionality with a style characterized by organic shapes, undulating lines and vibrant colours. From the wallpaper patterns to the plastic dustbins, the designer took even the tiniest detail into consideration in creating 42 rooms with a neo-pop aesthetic and a feeling of tranquillity and cool comfort. Utilities are discreetly hidden in cleverly designed spaces, whose transparent surfaces appear to dissolve for a more spacious and airy atmosphere. The five poolside bungalows overlook a giant mosaic shaped like an amoeba and a perpetually flowing waterfall, while the penthouse suites, enclosed by sliding-glass windows, command wonderful views from verandas as large as the rooms themselves of the Penteli mountains and the bustling city centre beyond. All rooms are lavished with the most up-to-date amenities, including plasma tellies and scrolling LED signage.

Special care has been taken with the lighting throughout the hotel, which changes imperceptibly from one hue to another, creating a luminous, otherworldly atmosphere. Works from Joannou's collection by well-known artists, including Jeff Koons, Tim Noble, Spencer Tunick, Christopher Wool, Claire Woods and Vanessa Beecroft, provide the finishing flourishes. For guests who cannot tear themselves away from the Semiramis experience, the restaurant-bar serves light snacks and more involved affairs all day from an extensive menu featuring Mediterranean dishes with a twist.

74 **Astir Palace Resort**

15 40 Apollonos
Rooms from €250

Located in a gorgeous natural setting on a private peninsula dubbed the 'Athenian Riviera', this palatial resort is only a 25-kilometre journey out of the city. The rambling property, covered with pine trees and commanding magnificent views over the Saronic Gulf, covers 75 acres skirted by golden sandy beaches, all of which contribute to the feeling of being far away from it all, while being only 15 minutes from the Glyfada shopping district and golf course (see p. 76), and 30 minutes from downtown Athens, the airport and Cape Sounio. The Astir (*astir* means 'star') has always been famed as a playground of the international jet set, including Ari Onassis and Frank Sinatra, and for hosting many of the world's political élite.

The site is comprised of secluded bungalows and three complexes (Arion, Nafsika and Aphrodite), each possessing its own distinct character. Refurbished in 2003, the Arion offers a more classical aesthetic, while the Nafsika is preferred by those with minimalist and modern tastes; both won awards in the 1970s for their revolutionary designs, courtesy of architects Voutsinas, Vourekas, Giorgiadis and Decavalas. The Aphrodite complex, built in the 1980s, is a quieter family affair. The rooms are spacious, with muted earth tones and extravagant marble bathrooms, many of which have incredible sea views. All of the rooms boast original artwork by contemporary Greek artists, including Alekos Fasianos and Dimitris Mytaras. The incomparable Presidential suite has 360-degree views of the bay and hand-crafted furniture inspired by ancient Greece, together with access to the fourth floor's Excelsior club.

Other pleasures on offer include taking a swim in the pristine waters of one of the hotel's three private beaches or a dip in the pool (both only a few paces from your room), or choosing between the seven restaurants on the property, including the beachside Taverna 37, the casual Kimata, the Sao Restaurant with its Polynesian menu, the upmarket Club House, and the ground-floor Gourmet Grill Room, serving Mediterranean cuisine in this spectacular island setting. A comfort zone you will never want to leave.

Periscope

22 Haritos
Rooms from €190

While some hotels promise to take you away from it all, Periscope does just the opposite. Located in the business, cultural and social hub that is the Kolonaki district, this hotel is ideally situated for immersing guests into the heart of the city. The hotel takes its name from a specially-designed periscope that allows visitors in the lounge to view the city from an 'urban surveillance system' on the roof that transfers images back to the lounge bar. A joystick controls a rooftop device that can be manoeuvred to provide varying views of Athens.

Periscope's concept and design is by DECA Architects, headed by Alexandros Vaitsos, and has taken the contemporary minimalist trend in urban architecture to its ultimate conclusion. The hotel's 22 rooms, emphasizing clean lines and simplicity, are spread across six floors. The ceilings of the 'Torpedo' rooms sport aerial views of Athens by artist Nikos Danilidis, while the four junior suites look out onto Mt Lycabettus and contain lighting fixtures that incorporate images of the city by day and night by Alexander Kuehne. The top floor is reserved for the Penthouse suite, which includes an open-plan sitting room and study, and exclusive use of the teak rooftop deck, complete with a Jacuzzi and splendid views of the Acropolis and Mt Lycabettus, extending as far as the port of Piraeus.

The outer wall of the building is the work of artist Yannis Ganas, whose work captures the movement of shadows cast by neighbouring buildings throughout the day, very much in step with the hotel's design concept of 'being in time' and capturing fleeting moments of the city, even if they are passing clouds. If you choose to lose yourself in the city via the lounge's periscope, you can enjoy the views from the comfort of chairs and sofas fashioned from refurbished Mini Cooper seats. Should you be startled by the appearance of a giant lobster or a stray chameleon strolling through the city, you have not had too much to drink; it's just a bit of animation by Pablos Germidis.

eat

Greeks have a distinct fondness for gathering around a table and sharing food, conversation and drink, and Athens offers an inexhaustible variety of venues to do just that; from traditional taverns and informal *mezedopolia* to cutting-edge gourmet restaurants, the pleasures and possibilities are infinite. Blessed with extraordinary ingredients such as its celebrated olive oil, Greek cuisine has many passionate devotees. In warm weather dining outdoors is a must, whether on rooftops, beside the sea, or under the stars, as is lingering for hours. Socrates himself observed that Athenians were given to describing sumptuous banqueting as 'having a bite to eat'.

44 **Edodi**

28 80 Veikou

This unusual restaurant, located in a restored neoclassical house in the Kokaki neighbourhood, has only eight tables in its three intimate dining rooms. A collection of small clowns and puppets adorns the tables and walls of the interior, with antique mirrors, chandeliers and wooden floors creating an eccentric domestic air. Attention to detail is paid at every turn, and the service is both discreet and personable; just don't look for a menu, because Edodi doesn't have one. Instead, waiters will present a carefully orchestrated procession of raw ingredients that will be used to create the dinner of your choice. The plate of local cheese with grapes and *glistrida* (purslane) is highly recommended, as is the medley of smoked eel, salmon and trout wrapped in aubergine with coriander for a delicate and distinctive starter. For the main course, the rabbit and langoustines served with sweet potato could inspire poetry. Desserts are light and fruity, allowing you to rise from the table satiated and content and (almost) guilt-free.

LEFT AND RIGHT

60 **Aristera Dexia**

17 140 Pireos & 3 Andronikou

A dramatic glass walkway showcasing the wine cellar divides this cavernous space, and gives the restaurant its directional name: 'left' and 'right'. Controversial designer Kyrios Cryton created a simple yet conceptually divisive interior, well suited to the inventive modern Greek cuisine of chef Chrysanthos Karamolegos. A native of Santorini, Karamolegos is known for his ability to transform even the most traditional dishes into something new and exciting. Co-owner Dimitris Litinas is behind the wine cellar, which has been named the best in an Athenian restaurant for five years running and boasts over 2,000 labels, 80 of which are Greek. Try the Ktima Alpha from northern Greece, or one of the Kir-Yianni wines from Naoussa, both of which go well with such meaty dishes as the tender beef filet in a dark raisin mustard sauce, or with the bolder seafood options like octopus with sun-dried tomatoes, olives and peppers, or baby squid in a lemon, chilli-pepper and coriander sauce. Jazz lovers will enjoy dining to some of the excellent live sessions played here regularly.

28 **Milos**

33 Athens Hilton, 46 Vassilissis Sofias

Milos has come full circle, returning to the place from which owner Costas Spiliadis initially drew his inspiration. Having first opened 20 years ago in Montreal and a decade later in Manhattan, the trilogy was complete when Milos came to Athens in 2004. Located on the lower level of the Athens Hilton, this vast minimalist space with its soaring ceilings and marble floors is centred around an open-plan kitchen. Resembling an outdoor market with fresh vegetables and a beautiful array of fish and shellfish on display, customers are invited to choose what they would like to eat. The quality of the ingredients supplied from all over the country is the main draw; fish is sent directly from boats on the day it is caught, and shrimp and langoustines are flown in from Chalkidiki, so fresh you can eat them raw. Shellfish includes *kidonia* (clams), *gialisteres*, and rare Greek oysters, served still squirming. Other specialties are greens hand-picked on Crete and Kythira, cheese from Santorini and Tinos, and *kakavia*, a rich and lemony fish soup, ladled out of a tureen at your table.

28 48 The Restaurant

One of the most visually exciting and highly acclaimed restaurants in Athens is 48 The Restaurant, established in 2003 by owner Theodore Margellos and located near the Panathinaikos football stadium and the US Embassy. Retaining much of its former warehouse-industrial design, the interior has been transformed by architectural firm Ioannou-Sotiropoulos-Van Gilder into a modern, minimalist space, with the dining room and courtyard separated by huge glass-and-steel doors. Arnold Chan (of Isometrix)'s sculpted geometric lighting niches illuminate the space with ever-changing hues of pink, green, yellow and blue. Outside, a wall of water flowing under the glass floor creates a dramatic atmosphere for summer dining. Cypriot-born chef Christoforos Peskias, who formerly ran Balthazar (see p. 129), has produced an imaginative alchemy in his cooking that results in a balanced mélange of flavours. This is the very best of modern Greek cuisine, with menus changing daily according to the availability of local ingredients. You would be wise to leave the choice of wine to omniscient sommelier, Yiannis Kaimenakis, who will suggest the perfect accompaniment to your meal from the outstanding wine list of over 500 labels.

When Alexandros Zoumboulis decided to make a profession of his passion and to convert his family's elegant mansion into a temple to food and wine for like-minded connoisseurs, he began by sourcing ingredients from the furthest reaches of Greece. The name of the restaurant means 'flavours of designated origin', and affirms Zoumboulis's commitment to seeking out the finest local products from the very best regional purveyors. Serious food aficionados will appreciate the meticulous preparation of each dish, and the resulting gastronomic experience of authentic Greek cuisine with a twist. The restaurant is also alleged to have the best selection of cheese in the city and offers, among many other varieties, aged *graviera* from Crete, *mastello* from Chios, and *ladotiri* from Lesvos. Be sure to take advantage of the well-rounded wine list, featuring predominantly Greek wines from the Vinifera wine shop next door. Owned by Zoumboulis's brother and knowledgable oenologist, Panos, it carries a comprehensive selection of vintages from all over the country. Gefsis Me Onomasia Proelefsis and Vinifera is a familial collaboration and celebrates the two proprietors' love of food and wine, which, like all good things, begs to be shared.

28 **To Ouzadiko**
15 Lemos Shopping Centre, 25–29 Karneadou

Unsuspecting passersby would never guess what treasures lie below in the calm, cool subterranean depths of this unassuming shopping mall. In the middle of the bustling Kolonaki district, To Ouzadiko has no outside sign indicating its location, nor does it need one. The cognoscenti know where to find it for some of the best *meze* in Athens. The dark wood interior with its marble tabletops is always full of Athenians, who flock here day and night for the delicious small dishes traditionally accompanied by a glass of *ouzo*, or *tsipouro*, another traditional spirit. With over 600 brands of *ouzo* and 72 types of *meze* on offer, owner Stella Perdika makes deciding what to order a pleasant dilemma. Some of the most popular specialties are roast suckling pig (cooked for 24 hours), butterfly-grilled sardines, and the many varieties of croquettes, some made from courgettes, chickpeas and tomatoes. The ingredients are always of the finest quality, bought fresh daily from the nearby market and prepared in Stella's small kitchen, to the delight of those lucky enough to secure a table.

SEAFOOD AND SUNSETS
74 **Ithaki**
17 28 Apollonos

Foodies setting out for Ithaki will find very fresh fish indeed, served up in a stunning setting. Built on three levels of wood and glass, the restaurant opens onto a beautifully landscaped terrace set into the cliff, with views over Vouliagmeni Bay and the Astir Palace Resort (see p. 100). A captivating location at sunset becomes even more magical as the night unfolds, and the sea provides a glamorous backdrop for a memorable meal. Although there are poultry and beef options, the predominance of seafood on the menu indicates the direction in which diners should veer. Choices include lobster-stuffed sole and langoustines in a light cognac sauce, along with marinated *gavros* (pilchards) with avocado mousse, but locals tend to like their fish plain, adding only olive oil and lemon. There are fish of all shapes and sizes, from *barbounia* (red mullet) to *rofos* (sea bass), which can be grilled, fried or baked. It is no wonder that the literature of the ancient Greeks on the pleasures of eating are devoted to the creatures of the sea.

14 Ta Kioupia
2 Olympionikon & Dexamenis, Politia Square

Ta Kioupia first opened its doors on Rhodes in 1980, serving recipes based upon the traditional cuisine of the island. This Athenian location in Kifissia followed in 1996, and today the restaurant is run by second-generation owner Vangelis Koumbiadis, who has taken an inventive approach to tradition. For the total experience, the tasting menu is a must. Diners can either help themselves from the procession of communal platters, or be served by attentive staff offering samples of some 30 different flavours, rather than courses. Savour this gastronomic journey in what feels like a medieval wine cellar, while taking in the sweeping views of the city beyond. Menus change with the seasons, but certain dishes remain year round, including *trahana* soup made from rooster and bulgur wheat, and warm aubergine and pine-nut salad assembled at the table. Lamb baked in vine leaves is also a favourite, as are dishes slow-cooked in wood-burning ovens and clay pots, called *kioupia*, from which the restaurant takes its name. For dessert, try the famous home-made *kadaifi* ice cream, or *mouhalebi*, a pomegranate-flavoured rice pudding.

ROMANTIC DESTINATION
Spondi
5 Pyrronos, Varnava Square

Universally acknowledged as one of the city's finest restaurants, Apostolis Trastelis's Spondi (which means 'libation') boasts a Michelin star and has been named to the Relais & Châteaux list. Under the supervision of chef Jacques Chibois, Spondi has maintained its reputation for cutting-edge gastronomy, making it a must for any serious foodie. The romantic lighting, barrel-vaulted ceilings, and original works of art all create an intimate atmosphere in which to appreciate the dishes to come.

From the moment the amuse bouche arrives (a potato soup swirled with spinach mousse and drizzled with truffle oil), you know that you are in for something special. Try fennel-encrusted scallops with anise, millefeuille pigeon filet with mushrooms served over crisp potatoes, or sweetbreads with truffles and chestnuts. The wine list offers vintages from both grand châteaux to small, local Greek producers. Whatever the occasion, dining at Spondi is sure to be an unforgettable culinary experience.

Mikrolimano in Piraeus is one of the Mediterranean's most charming and picturesque harbours, and is lined with small fishing boats and charming restaurants. Bypass the wily sharks attempting to seduce the uninformed into their touristy tavernas, and head directly for diamond-in-the-rough Jimmy & the Fish. Famous for its lobster-spaghetti-for-two served in the skillet, shrimp flambéed in *ouzo*, and octopus slow-cooked in red wine, to name but a few beloved dishes, the restaurant's long-standing reputation is based on its consistent quality and the freshness of its seafood. The service is impeccable, leaving you free to soak in the atmosphere and watch the sailboats, their multi-coloured flags fluttering in the wind, gliding in and out of the harbour with the island of Aegina (see p. 150) visible in the distance. Inside, the wood-panelled décor, accented with nautical antiques, creates a cozy atmosphere in winter, while in summer the seaside deck allows diners the sensation of having set sail for distant shores.

STARS IN THEIR EYES
74 **O Serkos & Tesera Asteria**
4 28 Xenofontos & Zepou

Devoted fans venture to the seaside suburb of Glyfada for this restaurant's extraordinarily delicious kebabs, made by the eponymous owner, an Armenian from Istanbul. The secret is in the lamb and beef mince, blended in-house to create a perfect balance of flavour. Some diners prefer not to tamper with the perfection of a classic kebab, while others opt for those laced with cayenne pepper, *kefalotiri* cheese, or secret-recipe marinades. The *asteria* ('stars') in the restaurant's name refer to family members who have contributed his or her own specialty; Serkos's son mans the grill and the wood-burning oven that produces steaming pitas, while his wife and daughter-in-law create platters of starters that include nutty fava-bean spread, a smoky purée of grilled aubergines, and the fiery *armenaki* salad made from hot peppers, onion, aubergine, tomato and cucumber. Desserts are home-made and rich, such as *kazantipi*, made the traditional way with chicken stock, and cheese-filled *kiounefe* with honey and shredded phyllo pastry. A family affair with great flair.

MICHELIN STAR
60
Varoulko
23 80 Pireos

With his distinctive style and imaginative flair, chef Lefteris Lazarou has changed the face of contemporary Greek cuisine at his seafood-only restaurant, Varoulko. Considered by many to be the best chef in Athens, Lazarou's innovative creations are made with simple Greek ingredients. The first Greek restaurant to receive a Michelin star three years ago, Varoulko has left the backstreets of Piraeus and is now located in Keramikos, the city's revitalized former industrial centre. In the summer when the roof is opened for al fresco dining, tables command magnificent views of the Parthenon. Let the chef surprise you with his tasting menu of unexpected combinations, including black-ink cuttlefish soup with crab and grouper cheeks, a sublime braid of garfish filet in a sauce of Corinthian grapes, and monkfish liver in honey, bay leaf and caramelized raisin vinegar. Dining at Varoulko is a superb culinary experience, best accompanied by a glass (or bottle) or two from the comprehensive wine list featuring many regional grape varieties.

PARTY ON THE JETTY
74
Istioploikos
19 Akti Mikrolimano

Istioploikos is named after the private Yacht Club of Greece, which is located in the harbour once known as Tourkolimano, or 'Turk's harbour', allegedly in reference to the Pasha's harem that bathed here. Today, the harbour is called Mikrolimano, or 'small port', and the restaurant is located right at the water's edge, surrounded by sailboats and humble caïques. Diners come to enjoy the nautical atmosphere and variations on classic Greek cuisine, including baked sea bream with braised greens, mussels *saganaki* (sautéed and served in a skillet with feta, tomato sauce and wine), and calamari stuffed with herbs and cheese. The café next door is essentially an extension of the restaurant, and is one of the most beautiful places in Piraeus in which to enjoy a coffee or cocktail. A canopied jetty stretches out to sea, and the views, on a clear day, reach as far as Aegina (see p. 150). At night, Istioploikos pulsates with a youthful crowd, who party to dance beats into the small hours of the morning.

FRANCOPHILE
74 **Septem**

13 58 Vasileos Georgiou B

One of the glories of a summer in Greece is discovering an exceptional culinary experience in a beautiful seaside setting. At Septem, you'll think it doesn't get any better. Chef Jean-Yves Carattoni's French influences have been somewhat Hellenized over the years, but certain dishes like foie gras with warm mango belie his background, while others preserve the flavours of the Mediterranean, including the succulent salt-crusted fish. Many of his more creative dishes hint at this Greek–French connection,

including the feta mousse with honey and black sesame. Place your trust in the knowledgable sommelier, Christoforos Christoforou, and you will leave with a greater appreciation for Greek wine and impressed at how far it has come in recent years. Those in the mood for dancing the night away can continue the evening next door with the beautiful people of Athens at the exclusive club Balux (see p. 123), with its trendy atmosphere and sleek design by Apollon Papatheoharis.

14
20

TURKISH DELIGHT
Tike
27 Kritis & Harilaou Trikoupi

Having crossed the Bosphorus from Istanbul, this Turkish restaurant has received an enthusiastic reception from Athenians. The contemporary décor is predominantly red and black, with jeweled lampshades, a mosaic fountain, and an imposing central grill upon which shish kebabs, heady with herbs and spices, sizzle away. *Ali Nazik* (minced lamb kebab on a bed of grilled aubergine and garlic yogurt purée), *Cherkez Tavugu* (chopped chicken in a walnut breadcrumb sauce), or *Kiodze Dogan-Sarmisak* (grilled onion with garlic and pomegranate dressing) are all superb. To accompany your meal, Tike serves a variety of breads and pitas baked to order in their traditional wood-burning oven, and brought piping hot to your table. Do save room for Tike's especially delicious dessert selection – if you must choose only one, the unique *Irmik Helvasi*, a warm semolina concoction concealing a surprising vanilla ice-cream centre, is a particular favourite.

drink

The ancient tradition of sharing food, drink and good company is alive and well in modern Greece. Domestic wines have come a long way, but most Greeks remain devoted to the anise-flavoured spirit (and national drink), *ouzo*. Athens' passionate café culture revolves around coffee and conversation, while after dark the city's nightlife is like no other. From May to October Athenians flock to the coast for dancing in beachside bars, whereas *bouzoukia* nightclubs are popular year round.

Café Avyssinia

7 Kinetou, Avyssinia Square

Tucked away down the narrow cobbled streets of the Monastiraki flea-market district is the charming Café Avyssinia. Avyssinia Square was named in honour of the king of Abyssinia after his visit to the area in 1844, and has a long-standing tradition of trade. Today the market is still an excellent place for browsing for antiques, second-hand furniture and unusual collectibles. Wedged in among the dealers, Café Avyssinia still serves Greek coffee prepared the traditional way in a *hovoli*, baked in hot sand in a copper *briki*. The word 'café', however, may be deceiving as Athenians come for more than coffee. Owner Ketty Koufonicola has a cult following who come to drink *ouzo* and sample her wonderful *meze* based on family recipes influenced by her native Thessaloniki, in northern Greece. Her creamy, white *taramosalata* is arguably the best in Athens; also recommended are the pork with prunes and spicy snails. On weekend afternoons, tables are placed outside in the square and old ballads and Greek love songs are sung to the accompaniment of an accordion in an atmosphere of a bygone era.

28 **Benaki Museum Café**

38 1 Koumbari & Vassilissis Sofias

Located on the rooftop terrace of the Benaki Museum (see p. 40), the café overlooks the National Gardens (see p. 46) and the Presidential Palace. Surrounded by so much greenery, it is easy to forget that you are right in the middle of the city. An ideal place for taking a break from museum-hopping (the Goulandris Museum of Cycladic Art is only a five-minute walk away; see p. 34), the café offers a small selection of traditional Greek favourites. Look out for the special of the day, which could be baked chicken with sesame seeds, or *lahanodolmades avgolemono* (cabbage rolls stuffed with mince and rice, in an egg and lemon sauce). There are also salads and other light choices, or if you are just in for coffee, you can pair your cappuccino with one of the sinful desserts. Well-known artist Antonis Kyriakoulis spices up the colourful menus and place-settings with humorous caricatures of café regulars. On Thursdays when the museum is open until midnight and admission is free, the café offers a special buffet supper.

DOLMAS AT THE DESTE

14 **Cosmos**

6 8 Omirou

On the ground level of the Deste Foundation (see p. 17) is this chic and artsy bar-restaurant, frequented by the upwardly mobile of the northern suburbs. Even the most discerning palates will find no fault with the creations (including pink Mojitos) of the experienced bar staff and intrepid young chef Dimitris Melemenis, whose fusion of Greek and Asian cuisines make for a wonderful culinary adventure in this lively setting. Delicately poached filets of scorpion fish (*scorpina*) atop lettuce-wrapped saffron rice *dolmas,* along with the salad with lobster medallions in vinaigrette scented with vanilla are highly recommended, as is the incredible dessert made from tomato and ice cream. The comfortable sofas and modern art make for a fabulous meeting place throughout the day and late into the evening, with the upbeat music becoming ever more clubby into the small hours.

74 Café Café
6 7 Zisimopoulou

Everything in this café, from the chairs to the lighting fixtures, has been conceived by top designers, lending the unmistakable stamp of originality to the space. The black sofas set against the white bar and the Corian tables are the work of Stavros Papagiannis and Giorgos Kiriazis, and lend a sleek and sophisticated air to the interior. The simplicity of Antonio Citterio's aluminium and fabric chairs blend well with Ingo Maurer's hanging lamps, which look more aesthetically sculptural than utilitarian. The décor is not the only draw, however, as Café Café serves up a fine selection of coffee, as well as many different kinds of tea, including classics like Darjeeling and Earl Grey, and green and herbal varieties. Located in the shopping district of the southern seaside suburb of Glyfada, the café is also an ideal place in which to drop in for an omelette or a light lunch of salmon tartare or grilled chicken *souvlaki* on a rosemary skewer, served with mushroom *plevrotos* and peppers *florinas*. The tart and creamy lemon mousse is also recommended.

VENETIAN PLEASURE
60 Bacaro
4 1 Sofokleous & 11 Aristidou

Across from the Athens Stock Exchange is the newly renovated multi-space Bacaro, which takes its name from a 19th-century Venetian phrase extolling the pleasures of eating and drinking in good company. Here the concept has been broadened to encompass all five senses through the addition of an exhibition space. A café-bar-restaurant-gallery in one, Bacaro also serves up nutritional fast food in the form of the famous *tramezzini*, light sandwich wraps made with soft, thin bread. The vaulted arcade is covered with a wood and plexiglass roof that floods the interior with natural light and allows views of the sky. Many of the features of the original building, including the mosaic floor, have been retained, while contemporary touches have been introduced, such as the graffiti-esque mural and works from art gallery Spilioti Projects. Exhibitions spill out from the gallery to create a dynamic backdrop to the café. The chef (he prefers 'cook') goes by the name of 'Mr Takis' and serves up local fare with a decidedly (and deliciously) Italian influence.

DANCE BY THE SEASIDE
74 **Balux**
12 58 Vasileos Georgiou B

Open to the sea and stars, this popular dance venue located along the coastal strip off Leof Posidonos attracts a youthful crowd. Set amongst a profusion of oleanders and palm trees, it features a swimming pool around which revellers dance to the sounds of R&B, house, techno, and the occasional 1980s remix. Guest DJs are flown in regularly from around the world, and create a high-energy atmosphere that keeps the party going through the night. The minimalist décor of this sprawling space incorporates such mood-enhancing details as glowing light fixtures and large beds enclosed in columns of curtains. A special cocktail bar offers over 200 mixed drinks, including the best Mojitos and Caipirinias in Athens. By day, the club operates as a private poolside café-bar, spilling out onto the beach. Beach bunnies can order a light meal, indulge in a bit of volleyball, or just admire the beautiful people of Athens, sporting bodies that could have been sculpted by Polykleitos himself. The complex is open from April to October, from early morning through to dawn.

GLAMOROUS BOUZOUKIA
60 **Athens Arena**
20 166 Pireos

Known already for his enormous glass sculptures, including the 'Runner' in front of the Athens Hilton, Costas Varotsos recently turned his hand to architecture and produced this massive *bouzoukia* nightclub. Quickly becoming one of the most glamorous destinations in town, the club features such names as Dalaras, Remos and Hadtzigianni, along with extravagant shows with outrageous costumes and a large number of flower-throwing fans. With a total capacity of 4,000 (2,500 seated and 1,500 standing), the club uses undulating glass booths to discreetly section off the teeming masses into private parties without interrupting the fluidity of the space. The exterior of the building is designed to resemble a starlit sky, a poetic allusion to the stars within. Athens Arena is part of larger project Pantheon, an enormous entertainment complex that will include other nightclubs, summer and winter cinemas and restaurants, all commanding fine views of the city. There will even be a helipad for jet-setters who just wish to drop in for the show.

OUTDOOR ELEGANCE

44 **Aegli + Lallabai**

2 Zappeion Gardens

Located in the National Gardens (see p. 46) is the elegant café Aegli, meaning 'glory'. A popular meeting place before it closed in the 1970s, it has recently been restored to its former glory and now serves as an entertainment focal point for the city's residents. The café also operates as a bar-restaurant with Mediterranean fare, oysters and, for dessert, gooey profiteroles and a mouth-watering creme brulée. Diners can take a seat inside or out, by the trees, and relax while enjoying the sunshine. Lallabai, Aegli's chic outdoor venue attracts a younger crowd in the summer. The city's first open-air cinema, in operation since 1907, is also located here. Whatever your mood, day or night, the park offers enjoyable outings for all ages.

ISLAND ADVENTURE

74 **Island**

18 27th km Leof Athinon-Souniou

The name suggests an evocative setting that will transport you to a beautiful Greek island the moment you arrive, and Island doesn't disappoint. Built on different levels, strewn with giant pillows, and decorated with low tables overlooking the sea, this sophisticated destination ushers in the gentle night breeze through billowing curtains, as candles flicker in ultra-romantic luxury. Bronzed beauties and their statuesque beaux sip summer cocktails while listening to chill-out house music, with the sound of waves gently lapping the shore in the background. It is worth the 30-minute moonlight drive from the city centre down the coastal route of Leof Posidonos to one of Athens' sexiest and most stylish venues. Those requiring more than liquid refreshment will find a restaurant that offers finger foods and Mediterranean cuisine. The ubiquitous Byzantine chapel found on most Greek islands is not absent from this 'island' either, making it a popular site for weddings, baptisms, and other occasions. This is one place where you are destined to fall in love.

28 Rock 'n' Roll

10 6 Loukianou & Ypsilantou

This club certainly lives up to its name, with a twist of glamour thrown in. Teeming with wannabes drinking expensive cocktails, wearing designer clothes and striking poses, Rock 'n' Roll is split into two levels: the restaurant on the upper floor boasts Olympian views, whereas on the lower level the bar snakes around comfy booths, overlooked by an extravagant chandelier. Should you venture here on weekends, joining the queue that stretches halfway down Loukianou Avenue, do make sure that you know someone who knows someone to get past the well-built gentlemen in dark suits at the door.

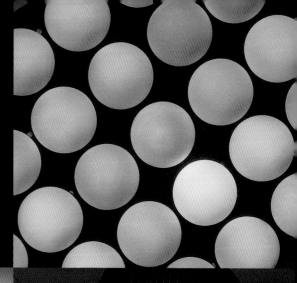

SPEAKEASY SOUL

28 Half Note Jazz Club

45 17 Trivonianou

Half Note is the city's top jazz club, but also features R&B, funk, and world music from Brazil to Senegal. Located next to First Cemetery in Athens' greenest neighbourhood, the club's atmosphere is reminiscent of the underground bars of the speakeasy era, with soulful serenades echoing across a crowded, smoky setting. While the décor of Half Note is traditional wood and stone, with photographs of the great and good who have graced its stage, the acoustics and lighting are ultra-modern. Open from October to May, with live music nightly, Half Note is always popular and reservations are a must.

RUM WITH A VIEW

28 Galaxy Bar (Hilton)

34 Athens Hilton, 46 Vassilissis Sofias

Perched atop the Athens Hilton and overlooking the city below, Galaxy Bar appears to hover at the end of the universe. Black floors embedded with sparkly mirrors and plush suede armchairs add to the glamorous and contemporary atmosphere, as do the pleated paper sculptures by the artist Pavlos. Cocktail aficionados will appreciate the selection of occasionally unusual spirits, from Louis XIII cognac to Zacapa rum, accompanied by caviar, sushi, or a fine cigar from the humidor.

Tucked away in the lofty heights of Kifissia between Mt Parnitha and Mt Imitos is this gem of a music bar, a favourite with Athenians for over 15 years. In the summer, the rooftop deck grooves to the sounds of jazz and 1980s pop, and partiers can slip away into one of the many cozy corners, cocktail in hand, and spend the evening in intimate conversation overlooking the shimmering lights of the surrounding hillsides. In the colder months, the indoor club, complete with turquoise-green interior, gets ever more boisterous as the night goes on. Should you have plans for later, you may want to make them tentative.

Around the corner from the St George Lycabettus hotel (see p. 92) is its casual bar-restaurant, Frame. In cold weather, Athenians come here for food and drinks, in this retro 1970s space with its funky furniture and psychedelic paintings. In the summertime, the action moves across the road to the canopy-covered garden. The wooden deck, sofas, colourful pillows and enormous chandelier, together with the DJ spinning tunes, create a party vibe that is somewhere between revelling and relaxing.

It is difficult to decide which is more beautiful, the people who congregate at Balthazar, or Balthazar itself. A veritable oasis set in a gorgeous neoclassical mansion in the Ambelokipi district, this bar-restaurant seems worlds away from the hustle and bustle of the city. Built in 1902 as the home of wealthy industrialist Alexander Pirris, Balthazar harmoniously blends history with discreet modern touches to create a sophisticated, yet relaxed setting. One of the loveliest spots in Athens, this romantic mansion is abandoned in the summertime in favour of its inner courtyard, with intimate sofas tucked away amongst the palm trees and lit by colourful, swaying lanterns. Visitors to Balthazar can lounge in the sensuous night air sipping Champagne cocktails or glasses of wine from the Peloponnesus, such as a white Moschofilero or a red Agiorgitiko. Those in the mood for more hearty fare can sample the deliciously creative Mediterranean menu of chef George Tsiaktsiras.

shop

For centuries the world has sought out not only the art and philosophy of Greece, but also its food and crafts, including olive oil, wild herbs, wine, ceramics, beads and gold jewelry, all making their way into the bulging suitcases of travellers returning home. And increasingly fashion-conscious visitors seek out up-and-coming Greek designers, who are making inroads into the international fashion scene with their individual designs that set, rather than follow, trends. Resistant to globalizing trends, the country is still full of idiosyncratic specialty shops in which browsing is as pleasurable as buying.

14 Fleria

■ 18 Dimitriou Vasiliou & Kodrou

Clever and aesthetically pleasing, artist-designer Nina Ioannidou's unusual creations bring together ideas and materials in unexpected ways. Her delightful designs often incorporate ordinary objects – from fruits and vegetables, to foliage and flowers – resulting in playful, humourous, and often surprising images with which to adorn one's home. A recent series consisted of paper vases decorated with faces from around the world, from which sprang eccentric flowers, and another, sporting unequivocally Greek images, was inspired by the 2004 Summer Olympics. Where else would you find an orchid growing out of an octopus, or an olive tree emerging from the *foustanella* of a traditionally-clad *Evzone*? Other motifs include sardines, dogs, cloves of garlic, classical architecture, and colourful tomatoes, cucumbers and lemons. Extremely popular for wedding receptions, Ioannidou's arrangements add panache to any occasion.

For over 50 years Eleni Vernadaki has been creating original ceramics that reflect her passion and intensity as an artist. Although many of her pieces look back to the pottery of ancient Greece, it is perhaps more appropriate to view her work in terms of inspiration, rather than influence, as her creations are transformed by her own genius into something unique and powerful, with more than a whiff of cult status hovering about them. Vernadaki's inspiration also seems to come from within, uniting both ancient and modern in one creative form. Unlike the ancient potter Euthymides, who inscribed an amphora with the pointed message 'Euthymides painted me, as never Euphronios could do', Vernadaki lets her pieces speak for themselves. Her style is unmistakably her own and her designs are bold, as is her use of line and colour, with poppy red, black and white, and the occasional splash of lemon yellow and midnight blue. All of the objects, from platters to bowls, teapots to candlestick holders, are as useful as they are beautiful.

This unique shop features products made from *mastiha*, the resin from the bark of the mastic tree, which only grows on the Aegean island of Chios, despite efforts to cultivate it elsewhere. Taken from the tree in crystalline form, amber mastic 'tears' fulfill their destiny at Mastiha Shop, near Syntagma Square, which has developed a wide range of products based on the culinary, medicinal, therapeutic and cosmetic potential of the resin. A line of traditional mastic-flavoured food and drink includes the famous apéritif *mastiha* (made with honey), *soumada* liqueur (made from almonds), *kaimaki* ice cream, chewing gum, and various desserts and biscuits, both savoury and sweet, as well as a range of gourmet items from pasta to chocolate. Numerous products exploiting the antimicrobial properties of mastic are used to prevent and treat such ailments as stomach ulcers, diabetes, and even cancer. Aromatic soaps and luxurious face and body creams produced in collaboration with the Korres cosmetic company (see p. 49) are also available.

14 **Free Shop**

15 Dimitriou Vasiliou

Free Shop began in the 1970s with a concept that echoed the spirit of the times: shoppers could bring items from home to the store and trade them in for new clobber. Out of this free-spirited exchange grew one of Athens' best-loved places to shop. In its 30 years, Free Shop has never succumbed to blink-and-you-miss-it trends, but instead offers pieces that become beloved wardrobe classics. From casual daywear to formal evening gowns, economical to expensive, the clothes for both men and women are made of wonderfully wearable fabrics from such designers as Eley Kishimoto, Martin Margiela, Balenciaga, Yiorgos Eleftheriades (see below) and Preen, along with the store's own brand. Free Shop's relaxed, friendly atmosphere and helpful staff will inspire you to part with both your time and your money.

60 **Yiorgos Eleftheriades**

28 13 Agion Anargiron

A strong presence in the phalanx of talented Greek designers, Yiorgos Eleftheriades is one of a growing number of trendsetters in the fashion world that are attracting attention both at home and abroad. Formerly located in Kolonaki at the Yeshop, Eleftheriades recently moved to the more vibrantly youthful Psyrri quarter of Athens. Here you will find his studio-atelier, with unusual prêt-à-porter pieces located on the ground floor and a boutique showroom upstairs. The avant-garde designs for both sexes emphasize cut and tailoring, and are unpretentious, uncomplicated and unconventional. Using only natural fibres (mostly linen, silk, cotton and alpaca wool), the designer's trademark is to create beguiling contrasts by blending textures, juxtaposing matte and sheen. Cool and casual yet discreetly sophisticated, Yiorgos Eleftheriades's clothes are comfortable, individual, and eminently wearable.

Orsalia Parthenis is following in her father's footsteps by creating designer clothes that are based on the same philosophy and quality that defined the label in Athens and Mykonos back in the 1970s. Using exclusively natural fibres, Parthenis keeps her devoted following by emphasizing casual simplicity. In today's increasingly hectic world when our daytime outfits often have to see us through to late in the evening, Parthenis's clothes have the added advantage of being both supremely comfortable and suitable for almost any occasion. Based on classic unisex lines, in a style often referred to as 'chic sportif', the designs are timeless and elegant, with luxurious weaves and textures. Until recently the collection has been tied to a monochromatic tradition, but is now embracing dusky plums, muted greens and luminous blues. Influenced by American sportswear of the Forties and Seventies, Orsalia Parthenis is innovative and open to new ideas, while remaining true to the label's origins.

Named after the famous fashion model of the 1950s, clothing store Bettina has all the class and finesse associated with the top designers that it stocks. Bettina has had a devoted following for over 40 years, attracting the patronage of both mothers and daughters drawn to the unorthodox mix of casual and formal wear. Designed for the sophisticated modern woman with an unconventional edge, Bettina's classic and avant-garde styles appeal to different age groups with different tastes and needs. With international names such as Comme des Garçons and Balenciaga alongside some of Greece's brightest stars, including Angelos Frentzos and London-based Sophia Kokosalaki, visitors to Bettina are spoiled for choice. Kokosalaki is particularly noteworthy for her fluidly sensual designs, with their pleats and folds that recollect the classical drapery of antiquity.

For over three decades Loukia has been designing extraordinary women's clothing that is both whimsical and theatrical. Her designs set aesthetic trends that are the last word in chic, and her styles never go out of fashion but instead become immediate classics. Loukia's background in costume design is evident in her creations, some of which incorporate dramatically flamboyant pleats and fluid swathes of luxurious fabric, while others are evocatively romantic and feminine, bedecked with ruffles, tulle and lace. Wearing one of Loukia's creations, designed for the confident, charismatic woman of the 21st century, will ensure that you do not go unnoticed. Those fortunate enough to be in the market for one of her bespoke pieces can visit Loukia's atelier in Kolonaki, and have a closer look at her exciting, often subversive, designs. While marvelling at the intricate embroidery work, you just might be inspired to indulge in a little fantasy about the glamorous circumstances you will find yourself in while wearing these beautiful clothes.

Those with a penchant for original and unusual millinery will be utterly taken with Katerina Karoussos's boutique, Planet Earth. Karoussos's evocative and extravagant designs are realized in the finest materials, whether straw, felt, or something on the more exotic side, and shoppers never fail to be charmed by her hand-sewn creations. Suitable for any occasion, from morning promenades to special events requiring one to be properly plumed, there are a myriad of styles to suit any taste and personality.

Beautifully beribboned wide-brimmed hats, lacy turbans and roguish berets are reminiscent of bygone eras, but all bear Planet Earth's trademark contemporary twist, whether a slightly turned-up back or a whimsical asymmetry. Karoussos also makes gloves, bags, belts and shawls in her cozy workshop, where a pleasant afternoon can be whiled away trying on hats to suit your mood, or succumbing to the temptation of ordering a delicious custom-made confection.

Near the Ancient Agora (see p. 54), the city's historic commercial centre, is Monastiraki, famous for its bustling flea markets, souvenir shops and antique dealers. Here you will find the incomparable Martinos, with its astounding collection of museum-quality antiques, housed over four floors of what was once the family home. Third-generation Eleni Martinos continues the tradition of overseeing this treasure trove that spans 5,000 years of history, from Cycladic vases to Roman marble statuary, to 17th- and 19th-century Byzantine icons. Many of these items are not allowed to leave the country, but alternative temptations are to be found, including pistols and ornate daggers, repoussé gunpowder boxes in silver, and 19th-century clocks decorated with Greek motifs, along with traditional coin necklaces and elaborate Byzantine gold earrings, with drops of emeralds, rubies and pearls. Martinos also specializes in embroideries, both Greek and Ottoman, as well as regional costumes. 19th-century portraits jostle for space with works by Lytras and other Greek artists from the turn of the 20th century, including Parthenis and Tsarouchis. A truly impressive collection that is well worth a visit.

One of Athens' most celebrated jewelers, Lina Fanourakis continues the over 140-year-old family tradition of creating exceptional, and highly original, hand-made works of art. Drawing inspiration from numerous sources, even nature's humblest creatures are transformed into superbly crafted objets d'art in 18- and 22-karat gold. In one collection of exquisite brooches, shapes are based on such unusual motifs as sea urchins, dragonflies and beetles, while another series, inspired by the Greek countryside, features poppies in white gold, encrusted with rose-cut diamonds, and evokes the transient beauty of spring. Some pieces are reminiscent of Mycenean techniques, including intricate gold bracelets and rings that are woven to resemble the pleated and folded fabric of ancient statuary. When worn, Fanourakis's creations seem to come alive next to the lucky wearer's skin. From the lavish and bold, to the intricate and delicate, there is no homogeneity of style, but rather an eclectic and enchantingly eccentric approach to design, imbued with the power of fetish.

Located where the most stylish shops in Kolonaki congregate is a one-of-a-kind, trendy hybrid gallery that is forging new roads into the art world. Housed in a charming neoclassical building that was once the residence of well-known poet Stratis Mirivilis, the building's original features, including the ceiling frescos and floor tiles, have been left largely intact. Millefiori Artspace's top floor is devoted to monthly exhibitions featuring some of the most important artists in Greece, while downstairs shoppers can find everything from books on contemporary art to designer apparel by such names such as Mother of Pearl, Lulu Guinness and Philip Treacy, along with hats, handbags, and Cutler and Gross sunglasses. The unique jewelry by Niki Paleochoritis is reminiscent of finds from Mycenae and incorporates antique Venetian glass beads, bone and unpolished rubies, while her more contemporary designs take the whimsical shapes of dragonflies, serpents, stars and hearts. Those who remember the childhood delights of playing 'dress-up' will enjoy lingering in this enchanting store.

One of Athens' brightest stars, this talented accessories designer has established herself in the world of fashion through the sheer audacity and originality of her creations. After international collaborations with companies as diverse as Levi and Absolut, who embraced her fetishistic flair, Syraka decided to place all of her wares under one roof and opened her first boutique in Kolonaki in 2004. Among her accessories are unusual purses, some made of soft, pleated leather with patterned silk, and others resembling fish scales or inverted Chinese fans. Most original and enchanting are the purses fashioned from old silver *tamata* (religious votive offerings) in the shape of flaming hearts. Once you have clapped eyes on the novelty evil eyes, necklaces, chokers and belts made of leather and crystals, embroidered rings, feather earrings, ponyskin bracelets and leather shawls, these boho-chic accessories become necessities.

28 **Kalogirou**

16 4 Patriarchou Ioakim

If you happen to be wandering about Kolonaki and notice a crowd longingly eyeing up a window display, you can be sure that the store in question is Kalogirou, Athens' premier shoe emporium. With two prime locations only a few minutes' walk from each other off Kolonaki Square, window shoppers are easily seduced inside by the covetable designs by top labels. From Prada to Ferragamo, Church's to Tod's, to Kalogirou's own label, discerning men and women come here for the finest shoes in the very latest styles. The shop's location inside a 19th-century neoclassical mansion covers four floors: the ground floor is devoted to handbags and accessories; the first floor to women's dress shoes; and the second to casual sport shoes. A separate entrance leads gentlemen to their own floor for classic styles from brogues to loafers, as well as accessories and travel items. The quality and selection ensure that for many Athenians 'Kalogirou' is synonymous with 'shoes'.

14 **Old Athens**

27 1–3 Argiropoulou & Levidou

Vassilis Zoulias has long been known in the world of sartorial chic for wearing many different professional hats, including fashion editor of Greece's premier woman's magazine, *Gineka*, fashion director for some of Greece's top designers, and consultant to many more on the international stage. In 2003 he launched a line of shoes and handbags that would have captivated both the romantically feminine Audrey Hepburn and more independent personalities like actress-turned-Minister-of-Culture Melina Mercouri. Zoulias's style exudes the aristocratic elegance of a bygone era, with enough tailoring to bring it bang up to date. His graceful lines are imbued with a contemporary flair for the unexpected, mixing a variety of fabrics with patterns from sassy tartan and polka dots, to sumptuous suede and snakeskin.

retreat

A sojourn to the islands and countryside of Greece offers landscapes of outstanding natural beauty only an hour or two from the capital. The country's topography is remarkably diverse, with stark rocky outcrops and lush green oases. Different regions also possess their own unique microcultures, comprising individual customs and history. The splendour of the surroundings, architectural ruins, local cuisine, blue seas and warm hospitality all make for an unforgettable experience that will convert first-time travellers into repeat visitors and ardent philhellenes.

The landscape grows ever more rugged and sparsely populated as you travel down the scenic Leof Posidonos towards the southernmost tip of Attica. Eventually you reach the Temple of Poseidon of brilliant-white marble , glistening in the sun on a windswept precipice. Built between 450–40 BC and dedicated to the god of the sea, this Doric structure is one of the most magical sites in Greece. Stop along the way in the tiny village of Legrena and visit Thodoros & Eleni's for delectable shellfish or, for a taverna with a view, turn off just before the temple to sample some of Mr Ilias's fresh fish.

Directly across the bay is Cape Sounio Hotel, discreetly nestled in the Sounio National Park and offering magnificent views of the sea and ruins. Here gorgeous sunsets can be savoured from the privacy of your own garden and pool in a luxurious setting harmonious with the wild landscape. Leaving your pleasure palace, follow the winding road 9 kilometres south from Sounio to Lavrio, an industrial town with a rich history dating back some 5,000 years. Some of the first

known coins were minted here, as were Athenian coins bearing an owl on one side and Athena on the other, dating from the late 6th century. Other ancient sites include the nearby Mycenean Tholos tombs, and the less well-known 6th-century Thoriko theatre – Greece's oldest – with its unusual oval shape.

Lavrio became one of the most important metallurgical centres in the world with the founding of the Compagnie Française des Mines du Laurium in 1875. The company was in operation until 1981, and left many of its industrial buildings and mining facilities behind; today it functions like an open-air museum. Development brought with it other advantages, and as Lavrio was the first town in Greece to have electric lamps and telephones (1880) and to be connected to Athens by rail (1885). Thankfully, the city's heritage is being protected with the restoration and conversion of many of its historic structures. Two hundred and forty-five acres of the old French factory has been transformed into the Lavrion Technological Cultural Park, which hosts exhibitions, conferences, seminars, and cultural and social events. The Mineralogical Museum preserves Lavrio's subterranean history with a display of over 700 mineral specimens, covering a bewildering spectrum of sizes, shapes and colours. To unwind from your adventures, take a stroll in the marvellous palm grove with its hidden café, Finikodassos, or find the old fishmarket and settle in at the *kafenio* (with no name), where locals stop in for an *ouzo* and a bite to eat. For a more substantial meal, try the humble but charming Panousis around the corner, one of the oldest and best eateries in town.

Lavrio's pace has yet to pick up, but change is inevitable. The port is already

being expanded to alleviate traffic at Piraeus, with ferry lines planned for the northern Cycladic islands. Until then, visitors can still rent boats from the Olympic Marina nearby. Alive with 5,000 years of history, Lavrio begs to be explored, remembered, preserved, and developed. Its unique monuments make Lavrio an exciting and alluring town, looking to its past to build its future.

Aegina: Country Life

- Temple of Aphaia Athena
- Agios Nektarios
- Ouzeri Geladakis (Fishmarket)
- Pansion tis Renas
- Proraion
- To Liotrivi Café Perdika

- Pilos kai Tehni Gift Shop
- Maridaki
- Konaki tou Vlahou
- Avli
- En Aiginas
- Mourtzis

Just half an hour from the mainland by hydrofoil (running every hour), the island of Aegina is considered by some to be a suburb of Athens, and locals often hop over just to have lunch by the seaside or for a swim. Although perfect for a day trip, the island warrants a longer stay to fully appreciate its charms. Despite its small size, Aegina was once a major naval power and a mighty rival to Athens in ancient times. Remnants of its former glory can be found just outside the main port at the rambling site of Kolonna, named for the single remaining column from the Temple of Apollo, dating from c. 500 BC, that protrudes sharply from the hillside. Local finds are housed in the archaeological museum, including a sphinx and funerary steles, whose carved figures inspired Rainer Maria Rilke to observe 'love and parting sit lightly on shoulders that seem to be made of a substance different than ours'.

The most spectacular monument is the well-preserved Doric temple of Aphaia Athena (the 'disappearing one') in the west, located on a pine-clad hilltop that commands fantastic views of the Saronic Gulf and its glorious sunsets. The road between the port and the temple passes through the mountainous interior of the island, dotted with the many pistachio plantations that yield Aegina's most important agricultural product. There are early Christian catacombs along the way, along with the medieval village of Palaiochora, once the capital of the island from the 9th to the 19th centuries. Built far inland to avoid pirate raids, this now-deserted village is a fascinating place to explore with its 20 ruined churches built into the craggy hillside. Across from Palaiochora is the ostentatious modern monastery of St Nectarios, dedicated to the first Greek saint to be canonized in the 20th century. Two other monasteries nearby are worth

visiting: Panagia Chrisoleontissa, dating from the early 15th century, and St Minas, where you can find cheese and sweets produced by monks on their own estate.

Returning to the main town via the island's other port of Souvala takes you past the house where Nikos Kazanzakis wrote his celebrated novel *Zorba the Greek*. Also en route is the Capralos Museum, with its fine collection of paintings and sculpture by the contemporary Greek artist, Christos Capralos. The entrance is marked by a giant bronze statue of the artist's mother, whose maternal tenderness was a recurring theme in his work. On this side of the island is Mouries, a worthy dining destination despite being well off the beaten track. In town, the medieval tower of Markelon and the former orphanage built by Capodistrias, now being converted into a vast cultural centre, provide an afternoon's diversion, as does browsing through the many shops lining Aegina's narrow backstreets.

Aegina, the first capital of the new Greek state, in many ways resembles other picturesque harbour fronts lined with cafés and tavernas, but as it is relatively free from tourists has an atmosphere all its own. Colourful floating stalls selling fruits and vegetables are interspersed between fishing boats, as horse-drawn carriages clip-clop down the street. It is easy to spend an afternoon doing little more than spending time at the traditional *kafenion* in front of the town hall, or mingling with locals at the modern and upbeat Yes café. The fishmarket is an obligatory stop for an *ouzo* and *meze;* it just doesn't get any more authentic than sipping an *ouzaki* and munching on the catch-of-the-day at next-door Geladakis as the scent of grilled octopus wafts down the cobbled streets. An ideal base in town (approximately 300 metres from the sea) is the 12-room Rastoni, where each guestroom is decorated in a different style with teak furniture and lovely private balconies. Nestled in a pistachio grove, Rastoni offers gracious hospitality and marvellous views over the archaeological site and the sea.

To the south of the island, about a kilometre out of town, is the Pansion tis Renas, a quirky place, with its old-fashioned iron beds, mosquito nets, and a sitting room that only seems to be missing a crystal ball, where you will feel more like a visitor than a paying guest. A further 9 kilometres south is the picturesque fishing village of Perdika, the perfect place for a seaside lunch. Cyclists will appreciate the pleasant and relatively flat ride from the harbour to town, and can stop off for a swim along the way at Marathonas, a happening beach particularly favoured by Aeginites. Once in Perdiaka, Proraion is a good choice for fish on the waterfront, with the cozy Liotrivi nearby for a coffee or drink. Nearby is the small beach of Kliedi with clear turquoise waters frequented by yachts in search of a more private dip. Shoppers can find local ceramics at Elleni Mourtzi's gift shop, and wildlife enthusiasts can venture further inland to a bird sanctuary where eagles, vultures, owls, hawks, swans, and even flamingos are rehabilitated for release into the wild.

When evening falls, there are many choices for dinner and entertainment, mostly concentrated in the main town. For seaside seafood there is the Maridaki, meat lovers can try Konaki tou Vlahou, and at Hippocampus waiters present you with a large tray of *meze* as soon as you arrive. For cocktails go to Avli, or 'courtyard', where you will soon find yourself knocking back drinks and playing backgammon with the locals, or head across the street for a hip alternative at Café Vartan, where you'll find a more intimate scene with lounge music providing a suitably chill-out background for sophisticated drinkers. For live music, head to the bluesy subterranean nightclub En Aiginis, which presents authentic *rembetika*, with many a patron joining in during the course of the evening, or the splashier Seaside Ellinikon, with an upstairs *bouzoukia* and downstairs club spilling out onto the front deck. Be sure to stop by Mrs Mourtzi's and fill up on locally grown pistachios and home-made pistachio sweets. Aegina is an island you will leave with a heavy heart and a vow to return for a little longer next time.

PINE TREES AND COBBLESTONES
Poros: Island of Two Halves

- Temple of Poseidon
- Zodohos Pigi Monastery
- Passage Ski Centre
- Hotel Sto Roloi & Anemoni Apartments
- Kathistos
- Primassera Restaurant
- Dimitris
- Bacchus
- Likiskos Bar
- Sorocco Club
- Sofrano
- Daglis Pastries
- Agapi, Monastiria and Vagionia Beaches

Poros means 'passage', or 'crossing', and refers to the narrow waterway that separates the island from the Peloponnesian mainland. Anglo-Irish novelist Lawrence Durrell claimed that it is impossible 'to exaggerate the charm of this little Aegean nook and the sense of elation it conveys', while poet George Seferis and Henry Miller were equally enamoured with the island, having spent summer days at the serene Villa Galini. Poros, with its cobbled streets, neoclassical buildings, and rows of traditional houses, is what one imagines a Greek island to be, and its picturesque tableaux of humble fishing caïques and villagers sipping *ouzo* while idly clicking their *komboloys* exude a tangible tranquillity.

Separated into two halves by a canal, the island is made up of Sferia, sheltering the town, and the larger Kalavria with its thick pine forests and sandy coves. The best way to see Poros is to set out on a rented bicycle, being sure not to miss the 6th-century Temple of Poseidon, where the orator Demosthenes poisoned himself in 323 BC rather than surrender to Macedonian invaders, or the lovely 17th-century monastery of Zoodohos Pigi, built near the island's only natural spring. Other sites include a deserted beach which contains the ruins of a 19th-century Russian naval yard. A five-minute crossing takes you to the sleepy town of Galatas on the mainland, with its famous *lemonodassos* (lemon grove) of over 30,000 trees and walking paths, including one to the Diavologefira, or 'devil's bridge', a natural rock formation that spans the gorge and the volcano of Kameni Hora, in Methana. Nearby is the Passage Ski Centre, while the Drepani resort combines ski facilities with family accommodation and a swimming pool. In town, step into the cool interior of the cathedral of St George to see the murals of Constandinos Parthenis.

Accommodation is provided by Roloi's apartments, in a restored captain's mansion, and Anemonie's converted farm houses; both options are cozy and intimate with period furniture and hand-embroidered textiles. Head to the excellent tavernas Kathistos and Primassera for fish, Dimitri's charcuterie for steaks, or Bacchus for its upmarket Mediterranean menu. Afterwards Likiskos provides the drinks, and Sorocco club the Greek and house beats for dancing to in front of lovely views over the sea. During the day Sofrano is a great place to consider your options over coffee with sweets from the closet-sized Daglis. The best beaches are at Agapi, also known as 'love bay', with shady pine trees meeting the sand. If you are in the mood for something more peaceful and secluded, head for Monastiria to the east or Vagionia to the north.

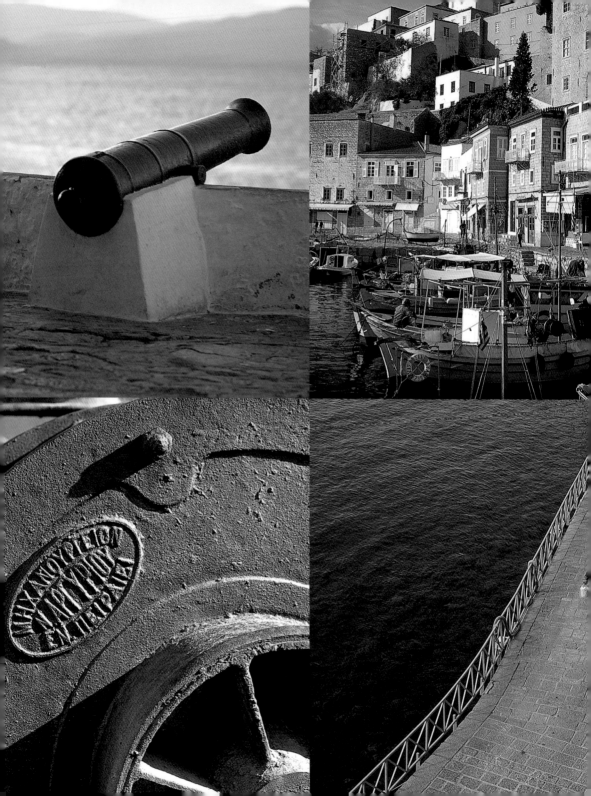

PICTURESQUE PORT
Hydra: Traffic-Free Paradise

- Historical (Istorico/Laografiko) Museum
- Hotel Bratsera
- Agios Nicholas and Bitsi Beaches
- Folk Museum (Lazaros Koundourioti)
- Elena Votsi Jewelry
- Taverna Gitoniko
- Sunset Restaurant
- Hydroneta Bar
- Pirate Bar
- Amalour

Only 38 nautical miles from Piraeus and 90 minutes by 'flying dolphin' hydrofoil, Hydra (pronounced '*ee*-dra') is a world away with its picturesque harbour-front town rising theatrically out of the sea. The urban character of Hydra grew hand-in-hand with its maritime prosperity, reaching its zenith during the late 18th and early 19th centuries when its commercial fleet ran the blockade during the Napoleonic wars. When revolution broke out in 1821 against Turkish occupation, wealthy sea merchants converted their ships for battle and spent fortunes for the cause, leaving behind a proud history and many beautiful *arhondika* (mansions) lining the harbour. To learn more about Hydra's illustrious past, visit the Historical Museum which highlights the island's decisive role in the War of Independence.

After a period of decline Hydra flourished once again with the growth of sponge fishing. The Hotel Bratsera, a converted 19th-century sponge-processing factory, allows visitors to experience the industry's history, and retains much of the building's former character and original equipment. The island was not rediscovered until the 1950s, when its appearance in a few popular films led to the arrival of a stampede of artists and intellectuals who moved in and are still part of the island's cosmopolitan social fabric. Retaining all of its evocative charm, Hydra has been carefully preserved; the banning of all motorized vehicles leaves only donkeys and your feet to get around with. Additional transportation is provided by water taxis that will take you to the many beaches tucked away along Hydra's coastline, including Agios Nicholas and the more secluded Bisti Beach.

Hydra is a walker's paradise; one steep climb through winding cobbled streets will lead you to the mansion of Lazaros Koundourioti, now a folk museum

with a public art gallery. Another peaceful, if somewhat strenuous, walk takes you to the Profitis Ilias monastery and the neighbouring convent of Agias Evpraxias, both offering fine views of the Peloponnesus. The harbour itself remains as it has always been: the focus of all activity on the island with art galleries, stylish boutiques, and unique jewelry shops like Elena Votsi right on the waterfront.

Whether you have worked up an appetite climbing up hills to monasteries, lounging on the beach, or shopping in town, you will find welcome respite at Taverna Gitoniko, which serves up some of the island's best traditional Hydriot cooking on its rooftop terrace. Alternatively, the appropriately named Sunset Restaurant is a wonderful setting for dinner and a view of the setting sun, or, if you'd rather chill out to classical music, visit the Hydroneta bar, where the atmosphere hots up as the stars come out. The harbour-front Pirate Bar, favoured by the rich and famous, could also become a regular haunt, or stop in at the Amalour, which is open year round with ethnic music and excellent cocktails.

Spetses: Wartime History

- Orloff Resort
- Hatdziyiannis Mexis Museum
- Bouboulina Museum
- Nafpigoxilourgio Shop (Mr Kobogiorga)
- Tarsanas
- Liotrivi Restaurant
- Dentrolivano
- Klimis Pastry Shop
- Throubi Bar

Spetses shares with Hydra a prosperous history of merchant shipping. It, too, played a significant role in the War of Independence, a proud heritage preserved in the island's suitably ringing motto, 'freedom or death'. In ancient times, Spetses was known as *Pityoussa* (or 'pine-clad'), a reference to the dense pine forests that still feature prominently in the landscape.

Your first encounter upon arrival will be the *Dapia*, or 'fortified place', the commercial centre of the island and former rallying point during the revolution. Past the cannons and cafés you will tread upon charming maritime-themed mosaics and, as there is a ban on automobiles, you can either keep on walking or rent a moped or bicycle to get around. Alternatively, you can choose a romantic horse-drawn carriage to reach your destination. Pause to admire the magnificent Posidonio hotel, built on the waterfront in 1914, before continuing on to the new Orloff Resort, a 19th-century mansion that has been converted into stylish suites with balconies overlooking terracotta rooftops and the sea beyond. Spend some time exploring the shore by taking a water taxi to Agii Anargyri, with its fine stretch of sand and excellent snorkelling inside Bekiris Cave, or visit the pine-shaded, emerald-green Zogeria cove.

To the west of the island is the Anargyrios and Korgialenios School, built in 1919 and modelled on the public schools of England. John Fowles was inspired to write *The Magus* during his years teaching here in the 1950s. Another site worth visiting is the home of Hatdziyiannis Mexis, Spetses's first governor, where the ground floor now houses an archaeology exhibit of items recovered from ancient shipwrecks. Other floors are dedicated to antiquities and artefacts from the War of Independence (1821–32), including the mortal remains of Lascarina Bouboulina, one of the revolution's most illustrious figures. Her late-17th-century mansion, with its carved Florentine ceiling, is also a museum displaying

such personal items as her ornate golden pistol and the safe from her ship, the *Agammemnon*, which she built herself and commanded during the war. Such is her legendary status – she is the only woman ever to be granted the title of Admiral – that Lawrence Durell wrote that even her portrait smelled of gunpowder.

More humble boats are still being built in the traditional way on the island, near the old harbour. You can pick up a hand-made miniature from Mr Kobogiorga, an occasionally grumpy craftsman who also makes models to order. In the harbour restaurants and tavernas, including Tarsanas, serve fresh fish, and Liotrivi, named after its olive press, offers Mediterranean fare in a seaside location. The quaint little Dentrolivano has an eclectic menu and is open year round, with tables in the square in summer and a cozy fireplace in winter. For desert go to Klimis, famous for its *amigdalota*, pear-shaped sweets made of almond paste. Nightlife on Spetses is lively and diverse; one place you won't visit for 'just one' is Throubi, whose ethnic, jazzy atmosphere will keep you there till late into the night.

Nafplio, Mycenae, Epidauros: Epic Adventures

- Akronafplia Castle
- Palamidi Castle
- Bourtzi (Island Castle)
- Nafplia Palace
- Bryon Hotel
- Arvanitia Beach
- Archaeological Museum
- Café Kendrikon
- Ellas Restaurant
- Vasilis
- Savouras
- Antica Gelateria di Roma
- Peloponnesian Folklore Foundation
- Metallagi
- Komboloi Museum
- Agnanti Bar (Fish Restaurant)
- Nautikos Omilos Bar
- Living Room (Likio Bar)
- Epidauros Theatre
- Ancient Mycenae

For centuries, the myths and legends of ancient Greece have drawn travellers to the legendary Argolid in the Peloponnesus. More recently this fertile land of olive and orange groves has become one of the country's leading wine regions, centred around Nemea, famous for its Agiorgitiko grape vines. Drive along the well-marked 'wine roads' and stop in for tastings at the many wineries along the way. Your destination is Nafplio, one of Greece's most beautiful towns with its majestic castles, elegant neoclassical architecture, and the indelible mark of Venetian and Turkish occupation in its medieval quarter.

Exploring Nafplio is a journey through the layers of its history. In ancient times it was the harbour for Argos. Abandoned by the Romans, the Byzantines later fortified the hilltop settlement of Akronafplia in the 12th century. In 1210 the town fell to the Franks, and was later occupied alternately by Venetians and Turks until the War of Independence, after which Nafplio served as the country's capital between 1829 and 1834. A hike up the 900-plus steps to Palamidi Castle, built by the Venetians, offers magnificent views of the sea and town, as well as of the Bourtzi, a floating island castle built for the protection of the port and to house the local executioner. Alternatively, ascend to the Akronafplia ruins James Bond-style by entering through the base of the hill, and taking the elevator to the foyer of the super-luxurious Nafplia Palace. Built by a government initiative in the 1960s by Papagiannis & Co., the hotel has recently renovated its bungalows to extraordinary levels of opulence with private swimming pools and stunning

views. Equally beautiful (and more reasonably priced) are the main rooms of the hotel which are being upgraded to provide the latest in technology and modern amenities in this unique historical setting. For a homier atmosphere seek out the Byron Hotel, a converted neoclassical mansion with rooms with a sea view. When it's time for a swim, head down to the pebbled beach of Arvanitia where Frankish fig trees, pines and oleanders line the edge of the turquoise waters.

Away from the café- and taverna-lined harbour, life centres around Plateia Syntagmatos, a grand Venetian-style square with an archaeological museum containing local Mycenaean artefacts inside the old Venetian naval arsenal. Stop for coffee at Café Kendrikon, or have a traditional lunch at Ellas restaurant. In the backstreets between the harbour and the square is a cluster of tavernas on Staikopoulou, where real home-cooking can be found at Vasilis and seafood-with-a-view at Savouras, right on the harbour. For something more upmarket, try the Nafplia Palace's Amimoni restaurant, and for a little taste of Italy drop by Antica Gelateria di Roma, where Claudia and Marcello Raffo serve over 30 divine flavours of gelato and sorbet, made fresh on the premises.

As you wander the narrow streets, stop in at the award-winning Peloponnesian Folklore Foundation with its wonderful collection of traditional costumes from all over the country, and a special exhibition on the production and use of natural fibres in Greece from 1835 to 1945. The museum also organizes periodic exhibitions and has an excellent gift shop. Nafplio is known for such eccentric and eclectic shops as Metallagi, which showcases the jewelry designs of Panagioti Alexopoulos and Maria Koutsoudaki, and has an open atelier enabling visitors to view the works in progress. The Komboloi Museum also has a *komboloy* workshop and retail store offering a wide variety of the traditional 'worry beads'. The lively Nafplio nightlife is a popular weekend draw for foreign visitors and locals alike. For romance, visit the restaurant-bar Agnanti at the edge of town, with tables along the pier and waves lapping at your feet, or the Nautikos Omilos bar next door, and for a more trendy club scene, head for the Living Room, off Bouboulinas Square, where the neighbourhood youth congregate.

Nafplio is also the perfect base for exploring two important archaeological sites: Mycenae (24 kilometres away), described by Homer as 'rich in gold', and Epidauros, with its superb theatre (30 kilometres). Mycenae was excavated in

the 1870s by Heinrich Schliemann, inspired by his obsession with the *Iliad* and the *Odyssey*. Wonder at the Cyclopean masonry of its citadel (so massive it was said to have been built by the mythical one-eyed giants) and the 'Lion Gate' with its two rampant lions, Mycenae's symbol of power. The most impressive tomb, the so-called 'Treasury of Atreus', dates to 1250 BC and originally contained such gold artefacts as death masks, breastplates, jewelry and weapons, which are now in the archaeological museum in Athens. Epidauros was the site of the important sanctuary of Asclepios, the god of healing and medicine, but is renowned for its splendid theatre, built in the early 3rd century BC. Set dramatically into the hillside, its remarkable acoustics allow even the drawing of a breath to be heard by all 12,000 spectators that the theatre can accommodate. Plan to attend one of the classical dramas performed here during the annual summer festival, for a memorable moonlit experience accompanied by an orchestra of cicadas.

Parnassus, Arachova: Winter Sports

- Santa Marina Hotel
- Panagiotas Taverna
- Platania (Taverna Kaplani)
- Emboriko Café
- Flox
- Aquarella
- Padre Padrone Restaurant
- Café Bonjour
- 925 (Paraskevi Kolobari)
- Raptis
- Paramount Restaurant
- Poliko Café
- Babis
- Athinaiko, Kelaria and Fterolaka Ski Centres
- Osios Loukas Monastery

Most people associate Greece with sun and sea, not knowing about its many superb winter destinations. For Athenians, Arachova and Mt Parnassus are obligatory sojourns that combine the charm of a traditional mountain village with the amenities of a trendy ski resort. Only a two-hour drive north of Athens, Arachova is the ideal base from which to explore the region, with the ski centre only 26 kilometres away and neighbouring Delphi (see p. 182) only 8 kilometres. Built upon five hills on the north slope of Parnassus, the village is renowned for its excellent cheese, wine and sheepskin rugs.

The Santa Marina Hotel, built into the side of the mountain, offers extraordinary views from both the breakfast room and the spacious private balconies of its guestrooms. Wood panelling, fluffy duvets and hand-made carpets create a warm atmosphere, as do cocktails in the fireside lounge on cold, wintry nights. Worthwhile distractions begin with sampling some of the local fare at the tiny taverna Panagiotas, at the top of the village near the church of St George, or try Kaplanis's Platania around the corner, another excellent taverna with delectable home cooking. Arachova is also famed for its nightlife, and favourite party places include Emboriko, a former deli now transformed into a hip destination; the more modern Flox and Aquarella, design-conscious venues with a splash of glam; and Padre Padrone, with its intriguing décor by Kyrios Cryton (see Aristera Dexia; p. 106). Located right on the main square, Café Bonjour has a loyal clientele and the best coffee in town, as well as croissants and pastries made on the premises by Nicos Korodimos. If you have a yen for some local jewelry, be sure to stop in at 925 and see Paraskevi Kolobari's unique

designs. For the best local products visit Yiannis Raptis at Elatos on the main street, and sample delicious sheep's-milk cheese like *formaella* or *mitzithra*, or stock up on regional produce including wine, honey, hand-made pasta, olives and sausages.

Leaving Arachova for Parnassus you will pass through the small town of Livadi, worth a pre- or aprés-ski stop for a snack in the chalet-style Paramount Restaurant, or for fireside drinks, coffee and home-made desserts in the more intimate Poliko, which is also popular for breakfast. A long-established taverna that features game on the menu is Babis, a venue that is big on flavour if somewhat lean on atmosphere. If you have not been waylaid by all the wonderful café-bar-restaurants and are destined for a ski area, there are three: Athinaiko, Kelaria, and Fterolaka, the latter two also with ski schools and shops for purchasing or renting the necessary kit. Gliding down the slopes beneath the majestic 2,457-metre summit affords magnificent views of the sea below, where the mountains tumble into the Gulf of Corinth. Parnassus is equally lovely in the spring and summer, and offers well-marked, wildflower-lined trails. One seasonal event worthy of note is the first Monday after Orthodox Easter, when Arachovites celebrate their patron saint with a three-day festival. Festivities begin when villagers, dressed in ornately embroidered costumes, process through town behind an icon of St George. Various contests are held, including a race between the village elders, cooking competitions, musical performances, and traditional dancing. Nearby is the 11th-century monastery of local hermit, Hosios Lukas ('Holy Luke'), architecturally one of the most important buildings of Byzantium, with its impressive mosaics and frescos and unusual octagonal dome. The beautiful location overlooks a valley of vineyards and almond and olive trees.

Delphi, Galaxidi: Centre of the World

- Treasury of the Athenians
- Delphi Archaeological Museum
- Maritime Museum
- Café Themistoklis
- Tassos (Fish Taverna)
- Maritsa
- Ydrohos Café-Bar
- Liotrivi
- Cosmas Dimitriadis (Jewelry)
- Hotel Ganimede
- Nikotakis

When Zeus sent two eagles to find the centre of the Earth, the birds met over Delphi, thus marking the site as the *omphalos*, or 'navel' of the world. It was here, amidst the precipitous cliffs and plunging gorges between Mt Parnassus and the Gulf of Itea, that the cult of Apollo was established, with devotees arriving from far and wide to seek the advice of the oracle of Delphi. At the sanctuary of Athena Pronaia is one of the great masterpieces of ancient architecture, the circular Tholos temple, dating from the 4th century BC. As you walk up the sacred way to the great Temple of Apollo, it is easy to imagine the proverbs once inscribed upon it, including 'know thyself' and 'nothing in excess', and the countless devotional statues that once stood here. Admire the reconstructed Treasury of the Athenians nearby, and continue up the hillside to the impressive stadium and theatre. Highlights of Delphi's Archaeological Museum include the extraordinary bronze charioteer, the enigmatic 'Column of the Dancers', carvings from the Siphnian Treasury, and the sculpture of the youth Antinoos.

Your next destination is the enchanting seaside town of Galaxidi, only half an hour away. Along the steep, zig-zag road you'll pass through the largest olive plantation in Greece. Sheltered in the Bay of Krisa, with lovely views of snowy Mt Parnassus, the town is full of beautiful 19th-century neoclassical buildings. The Maritime Museum documents the community's glory days after the War of Independence, in which the Galaxidiotes made a significant contribution in the form of their formidable naval power. There is a splendid collection of paintings of Galaxidis ships from the 19th and 20th centuries, along with wooden figureheads, nautical equipment, and local antiquities. The transition from sail to steam signalled the end of Galaxidi's fortunes, and the town subsequently slid into economic decline.

NAUTICAL HISTORICAL MUSEUM OF GALAXIDI

A leisurely stroll along the harbour front will acquaint you with the local scene. Begin at Café Themistoklis, which dates back to the 1860s and is now run by fourth-generation proprietor Thanasis Kamvysis, and welcomes you with an atmosphere redolent with the salty tales of sea captains who once swapped adventures by the fire. You can choose to dine between two neighbouring eateries, the humble fish taverna Tassos, with its delicious langoustines, or the more upmarket Maritsa, Galaxidi's version of Lloyds of London, where shipbuilders, owners and captains would congregate to conduct business and socialize. For 20 years Maritsa has been serving up her specialty chicken and courgette pies, and shrimp with orzo baked in clay, together with her signature mussels with rice. Further along diners can stop in for a drink at Ydrohos, or continue to the second port where Liotrivi, a former olive press has been converted into a café and gallery exhibiting artist-owner Minas's paintings of the local landscape. Visit goldsmith Cosmas Dimitriadis's jewelry shop for designs passed down from his father and grandfather, as well as daughter Arianna's more contemporary pieces. Under Dimitriadis's tenure as president of the town's cultural foundation, the last windmill visible on the hill overlooking

Galaxidi has been restored and converted into a museum on the history of breadmaking.

Chrisoula and Kostas Papalexi are the gracious proprietors of Hotel Ganimede, a nine-room budget pensione occupying a newly renovated 19th-century house that in its former life belonged to a sea captain. The cozy rooms are furnished with wrought-iron beds, and topped with high wooden ceilings. Sumptuous breakfasts of fresh juice, home-made jam, cake, chutney, and anything else your heart might desire are served in the garden. Those undefeated by the Ganimede breakfast experience should head for nearby Nikotakis and its decadent local pastries.

contact

All telephone numbers are given for dialling locally. From abroad, the country code is +30, followed by the number below. The number in brackets by the name is the page number on which the entry appears.

48 The Restaurant [142]
48 Armatolon & Klefton
Ampelokipi 11471 Athens
T   210 645 0658
E   48_ilta@otenet.gr
W   www.48therestaurant.com

ADC Eleni Vernadaki [133]
4 Valaoritou
Kolonaki, Athens
T   210 361 0194

Aegli [124]
Zappeion Gardens
10557 Athens
T   210 336 9300
F   210 325 2952
W   www.aeglizappiou.com

Afternoon [30]
1 Dinokratous, Plateia Dexameni
Kolonaki, Athens
T   210 722 5380
F   210 729 0439

**Agios Nikolaos
Raganvas** [50]
1 Pritaniou
Plaka 10556 Athens
T   210 322 8193

Akrotiri [76]
5 Vasileos Georgiou B
Agios Kosmas

Kalamaki 10677 Athens
T   210 985 9147
F   210 985 9149
E   info@akrotirilounge.gr
W   www.akrotirilounge.gr

Amalthia Galactopolio [50]
16 Tripodon
Plaka, Athens
T   210 322 4635

Ancient Agora [54]
24 Adrianou
Monastiraki, Athens
T   210 321 0185

Arhaion Gefsis [65]
22 Kodratou
Metaxourgio, Athens
T   210 523 9661

Aristera Dexia [106]
140 Pireos & 3 Andronikou
Rouf, Athens
T   210 342 2380/2606
E   info@aristeradexia.gr
W   www.aristeradexia.gr

Aristokratikon [47]
9 Karagiorgi Servias
Syntagma 10563 Athens
T   210 322 0546
F   210 360 3784
W   www.aristokratikon.com

Ariston [46]
10 Voulis
Syntagma, Athens

Astir Palace Resort [100]
40 Apollonos
Vouliagmeni 16671 Athens
T   210 890 2000
F   210 896 2582
E   reservation@astir.gr
W   www.astir-palace.gr

Astrolavos Artlife [37]
11 Irodotou
Kolonaki 10674 Athens
T   210 722 1200
F   210 722 1304
E   gallery@astrolavos.gr
W   www.astrolavos.gr

Athens Arena [123]
166 Pireos
11854 Athens
T   210 347 1111
E   info@athenspantheon.com
W   www.athenspantheon.com

**Athens Concert Hall
(Megaron Mousikis)** [40]
1 Kokkali & Vassilissis Sofias
11521 Athens
T   210 728 2333
F   210 729 0174
W   www.megaron.gr

Athinais [69]
34–36 Kastorias
Votanikos 10447 Athens
T   210 348 0000
F   210 348 0007
E   athinais@athinais.com.gr
W   www.athinais.com.gr

Bacaro [122]
1 Sofokleous & 11 Aristidou
10559 Athens
T   210 321 1882
F   210 321 1884
E   info@bacaro.gr
W   www.bacaro.gr

Balthazar [129]
27 Veranzerou
Ambelokipi, Athens
T   210 644 1215
W   www.balthazar.gr

Balux [123]
58 Vasileos Georgiou B
Glyfada 16674 Athens
T   210 894 1620
F   210 894 1189
E   escape@balux-septem.com
W   www.balux-septem.com

Benaki Museum [40]
1 Koumbari & Vassilissis Sofias
Kolonaki 10674 Athens
T   210 367 1000

F   210 367 1063
E   benaki@benaki.gr
W   www.benaki.gr

Benaki Museum of Islamic Art [62]
22 Agion Asomaton & 12 Dipylou
Keramikos 11854 Athens
T   210 325 1311
F   210 322 5550
W   www.benaki.gr

Benaki Museum Pireos Annexe [69]
138 Pireos & Andronikou
Votanikos 11854 Athens
T   210 345 3111
F   210 345 3743
E   benaki@benaki.gr
W   www.benaki.gr

Bettina [135]
40 Pindarou &
29 Anagnostopoulou
Kolonaki 10673 Athens
T   210 339 2094
F   210 339 2082

The Boboniera [24]
12 Papadiamanti
Kifissia, Athens
T   210 801 9687

Café Avyssinia [120]
7 Kinetou, Avyssinia Square
Monastiraki 10555 Athens
T/F 210 321 4047
W   www.avissinia.gr

Café Café [122]
7 Zisimopoulou
Glyfada Athens
T   210 894 4996

Café Waichhart [83]
58 Akti Moutsopoulou
Piraeus 18546 Athens
T   210 453 4408

Cava Anthidis [39]
13–15 Ypsilantou
Kolonaki 54248 Athens
T   210 721 7630
F   210 723 1963

Cava Cellier [39]
31 Patriarchou Ioakim
Kolonaki 10675 Athens
T   210 729 8330
F   210 729 8331
E   cellier@genkacomm.gr
W   www.cellier.gr

Celia Kritharioti [50]
8 Dedalou
Plaka 10558 Athens
T   210 323 0689
W   www.celiakritharioti.gr

Cosmos [121]
8 Omirou
N. Psychiko 15451 Athens
T   210 672 9150
F   210 672 9154
E   cocktail@hellasnet.gr
W   www.cosmos-bar.gr

Danos [78]
61 Kyprou
Glyfada 16674 Athens
T   210 968 0629
F   210 968 0769

Deste Foundation [17]
8 Omirou
N. Psychiko, Athens
T   210 672 9460
F   210 672 9470
E   info@deste.gr
W   www.deste.gr

Dioscouri [53]
13 Dioskouron
Monastiraki, Athens
T   210 321 9607

Diporto [65]
9 Sofokleous & Theatrou
Omonia, Athens
T   210 321 1463

Domaine Harlaftis [24]
11 Stamatas
Stamata 14565 Athens
T   210 621 9374/6546
F   210 621 9290
E   wines@harlaftis.gr
W   www.harlaftis.gr

Duende [57]
2 Tziraion & 3 Dionisou
Areopagitou
Syntagma, Athens
T   210 924 7069

Edodi [106]
80 Veikou
Koukaki 11741 Athens
T/F 210 921 3013

Eleftheroudakis [49]
17 Panepistimiou
10564 Athens
T   210 325 8440
F   210 323 9821
E   elebooks@books.gr
W   www.books.gr

Elena Syraka [140]
21 Loukianou
Kolonaki 10675 Athens
T   210 722 0113
F   210 724 9052

Elixir [65]
41 Evripidou
10554 Athens

T   210 321 5141
F   210 321 5148
E   elixir@otenet.gr

En Delphis [34]
5 Delfon
Kolonaki, Athens
T   210 360 8269
W   www.endelphis.gr

Fanourakis [139]
23 Patriarchou Ioakim
Kolonaki 10675 Athens
T   210 721 1762
F   210 724 6432
E   fanourakis@altecnet.gr
W   www.fanourakis.gr

Filion [34]
34 Skoufa
Kolonaki 10672 Athens
T   210 360 8468
F   210 361 2850

Filistron [57]
23 Apostolou Pavlou
Thisio, Athens
T   210 346 7554
E   info@filistron.com
W   www.filistron.com

Fleria [132]
18 Dimitriou Vasiliou & Kodrou
N. Psychiko, Athens
T   210 675 3480
F   210 675 3442
E   fleria@fleria.gr
W   www.fleria.gr

Frame [128]
1 Dinokratous, Plateia Dexameni
Kolonaki, Athens
T   210 721 4368

Free Shop [134]
15 Dimitriou Vasiliou
N. Psychiko, Athens
T   210 675 4308
E   mail@freeshop.com.gr
W   www.freeshop.com.gr

Fresh [17]
162 Kifissias
Psychiko, Athens
T   210 675 3802

Fresh Hotel [88]
26 Sofokleous
10552 Athens
T   210 524 8511
F   210 524 8517
E   info@freshhotel.gr
W   www.freshhotel.gr

Frissiras Museum [50]
3 & 7 Monis Asteriou
Plaka 10558 Athens
T   210 323 4678

F   210 331 6027
E   info@frissirasmuseum.com
W   www.frissirasmuseum.com

Gaia Centre [20]
100 Othonos
Kifissia 14562 Athens
T   210 801 5870
F   210 808 0674
E   goul@gnhm.gr
W   www.gnhm.gr

Galaxy [49]
10 Stadiou
Syntagma, Athens
T   210 322 7733

Galaxy Bar (Hilton) [127]
Athens Hilton
46 Vassilissis Sofias
Kolonaki 11528 Athens
T   210 728 1000
W   www.hilton.co.uk/athens

Gazarte [69]
32–34 Voutadon
Gazi, Athens
T   210 346 0347
E   info@gazarte.gr
W   www.gazarte.gr

Gefsis Me Onomasia Proelefsis [109]
317 Kifissias
Kifissia, Athens
T   210 800 1402

Glyfada Golf Club [76]
Terma Pronois
P.O. Box 70034
Glyfada 16610 Athens
T   210 894 6820
F   210 894 3721
E   glyfgolf@internet.gr
W   www.glyfadagolf.gr

Goulandris Museum of Cycladic Art [34]
4 Neofytou Douka
Kolonaki 10674 Athens
T   210 722 8321
F   210 723 9382
E   info@cycladic-m.gr
W   www.cycladic-m.gr

Goulandris Museum of Natural History [20]
13 Levidou
Kifissia 14562 Athens
T   210 801 5870
F   210 808 0674
E   goul@gnhm.gr
W   www.gnhm.gr

Goutis [30]
10 Dimokritou
Kolonaki, Athens
T   210 361 3557

Hadzilias [47]
21 Voulis
Syntagma, Athens
T   210 321 9591

Hadzis [17]
196 Kifissias
N. Psychiko, Athens
T   210 674 7011
F   210 677 5398

Half Note Jazz Club [127]
17 Trivonianou
Mets 11636 Athens
T   210 921 3310
F   210 921 3311
W   www.halfnote.gr

Harris & Angelos [39]
18 Voukourestiou
Kolonaki 10671 Athens
T   210 362 1060

Hotel Grande Bretagne [90]
Syntagma Square
Syntagma 10563 Athens
T   210 333 0000
F   210 322 8034
E   info@grandebretagne.gr
W   www.grandebretagne.gr

Ideal [62]
46 Panepistimiou
Omonia 10678 Athens
T   210 330 3000

**Ileana Tounta
Contemporary Art
Centre** [40]
48 Armatolon & Klefton
Kolonaki 11471 Athens
T   210 643 9466
F   210 644 2852
E   ileanatounta@art-tounta.gr
W   www.art-tounta.gr

**Ilias Lalaounis Jewelry
Museum** [57]
12 Karyatidon & Kallisperi
11742 Athens
T   210 922 1044
F   210 923 7358
E   jewelrymuseum@ath.
forthnet.gr
W   www.lalaounis-
jewelrymuseum.gr

Ionia [76]
23 Grigoriou Lambraki
Glyfada, Athens
T   210 259 3600
F   210 898 5907
W   www.ionia.gr

Irene [23]
57 Thiseos
Ekali, Athens
T   210 622 9226

Island [125]
27th km Leof Athinon-Souniou
Varkiza 16672 Athens
T   210 892 5000
F   210 892 5050
E   sales@island-central.gr
W   www.island-central.gr

Istioploikos [115]
Akti Mikrolimano
Piraeus 18532 Athens
T   210 413 4084
F   210 413 4086
E   info@istioploikos.gr
W   www.istioploikos.gr

Ithaki [111]
28 Apollonos
Vouliagmeni, Athens
T   210 896 3747

Jimmy & the Fish [114]
46 Alexandrou Koumoundourou
Piraeus, Athens
T   210 412 4417
E   info@jimmyandthefish.gr
W   www.jimmyandthefish.gr

Kalogirou [141]
4 Patriarchou Ioakim
Kolonaki, Athens
T   210 335 6401
F   210 335 6451
E   info@lemonis.gr
W   www.lemonis.gr

Kariofillis [36]
1 Staikou
Kolonaki 10680 Athens
T   210 3617343

Katerina Psoma [52]
18 Pritaniou
Plaka 10556 Athens
T/F 210 331 7912
E   info@katerinapsoma.gr
W   www.katerinapsoma.gr

Kitrino Podilato [66]
116 Keramikou & Iera Odos
Gazi, Athens
T   210 346 5830

Koan Bookstore [40]
5 Delfon
Kolonaki 10680 Athens
T   210 362 8265
F   210 362 8307

Kollias [83]
3 Stratigou Plastira
Piraeus 17856 Athens
T   210 462 9620
F   210 461 9150

Kombologadiko [36]
6 Koumbari
Kolonaki, Athens

T   210 362 4267
F   210 723 7103
E   info@kombologadiko.gr
W   www.kombologadiko.gr

Korres [49]
8 Ivikou & Eratosthenous
Pangrati 11635 Athens
T   210 722 2774
F   210 756 2122
E   info@korres.com
W   www.korres.com

Krinos [65]
87 Aiolou
Omonia, Athens
T   210321 6852

Krisa Gi [18]
23 Agiou Konstantinou
Maroussi, Athens
T   210 8056666

Lambros [78]
20 Posidonos
Vouliagmeni, Athens
T   210 896 0144
F   210 896 1829

Liana Vourakis [37]
42 Pindarou
Kolonaki 10673 Athens
T   210 361 9441
F   210 361 7703

Life Gallery Athens [96]
103 Thiseos
Ekali 14565 Athens
T   210 622 0400
F   210 622 9353
E   info-lifegallery@bluegr.com
W   www.bluegr.com

Lolos Ski Centre [80]
Vouliagmeni Yacht Club
Vouliagmeni, Athens
T   210 896 4414
E   skiouga@otenet.gr

Loukia [136]
24 Kanari
Kolonaki 10674 Athens
T   210 362 7334
F   210 362 5097
E   loukiab@netscape.net

Mamacas [66]
41 Persophones
Gazi, Athens
T   210 346 4984
F   210 341 3815
E   mamacas@otenet.gr
W   www.mamacas.gr

Mandragoras [83]
14 Gounaris
Piraeus 18531 Athens
T   210 417 2961/210 422 0319

F   210 4119467
E   mandraoras@otenet.gr
W   www.mandragoras.gr

**Marianna Petridi
Jewelry** [30]
34 Haritos
Kolonaki, Athens
T/F 210 721 7789
E   petrimar@otenet.gr

Martinos [138]
50 Pandrossou
Plaka 10555 Athens
T   210 321 3110
E   martino1@otenet.gr
W   www.martinisart.gr

Mastiha Shop [133]
6 Panepistimiou & Kriezotou
Syntagma 10671 Athens
T   210 363 2750
F   210 363 1850
E   info@matihashop.com
W   www.mastihashop.com

Medusa Art Gallery [30]
7 Xenokratous
Kolonaki 10675 Athens
T   210 724 4552
F   210 722 3605
E   medusa9@otenet.gr
W   www.medusaartgallery.com

Melissinos [70]
2 Agia Theklasi
Psyrri, Athens

Mesogaia [49]
52 Nikis & Kydathinaion
Plaka 105 58 Athens
T   210 322 9146
F   210 322 9147
E   mesogaia@otenet.gr

Mihalarias Art [24]
260 Kifissias & Diligianni
Kifissia 14562 Athens
T   210 623 4320
F   210 623 0928
E   mihalarias@internet.gr

Millefiori Artspace [140]
29 Haritos
Kolonaki 10675 Athens
T   210 7239558
F   210 7231964
E   millefioriartspace@yahoo.com

Milos [107]
Athens Hilton
46 Vassilissis Sofias
Kolonaki 11528 Athens
T   210 724 4400
F   210 724 4411
E   milos@info.ca
W   www.milos.ca

Mokka [62]
44 Athinas
10551 Athens
T/F 210 325 1311
E nikpsom@yahoo.com
W www.mokka.gr

National Gardens [46]
Irodou Attikou
Syntagma 10563 Athens

**National Museum of
Contemporary Art** [40]
Athens Concert Hall
1 Kokkali & Vassilissis Sofias
11521 Athens
T 210 924 2111
F 210 924 5200
E protocol@emst.culture.gr
W www.emst.gr

O Serkos & 4 Asteria [114]
28 Xenofontos & Zepou
Glyfada 16675 Athens
T 210 964 9553

**Odeon of Herodes
Atticus** [49]
Dionisou Areopagitou
Athens
T 210 323 2771
W www.culture.gr

Old Athens [141]
1–3 Argiropoulou & Levidou
Kifissia, Athens
T 210 801 7023

Opus [34]
25 Tsakalof
Kolonaki 10673 Athens
T 210 361 2356
F 210 360 6210
E opusdeco@otenet.gr

Palia Agora [18]
26 Kehagia & M. Renieri
Filothei, Athens
T 210 683 7037
W www.specialcoffee.com/
paliaagora

Papadakis Restaurant [34]
15 Fokilidou
Kolonaki, Athens
T 210 360 8621

The Park Restaurant [39]
Eleftherias Park
Vassilissis Sofias
11521 Athens
T 210 722 3784
F 210 722 3724
E info@toparko.gr
W www.toparko.gr

Parthenis [135]
20 Dimokritou & Tsakalof
Kolonaki, Athens
T 210 271 3844
F 210 272 3682
E orsa@ath.forthnet.gr

Pentheroudakis [39]
19 Voukourestiou
Kolonaki, Athens
T 210 361 3187
F 210 360 8019
W www.atlantis.gr/
pentheroudakis

Pere Ubu [79]
74 Kyprou
Glyfada, Athens
T 210 894 1450
E food_concepts@pathfinder.gr

Periscope [102]
22 Haritos
Kolonaki 10675 Athens
T 210 729 7200
F 210 729 7206
E info@periscope.gr
W www.periscope.gr

Perivoli t'Ouranou [53]
19 Lyisikratous &
50 Leof Vassilissis Amalias
Plaka 10558 Athens
T 210 323 5517
W www.perivoli-touranou.gr

Piperia Seafood [17]
8 Angelos Sikelianou & Adrianiou
N. Psychiko 11525 Athens
T 210 672 9114
E info@piperia-seafood.gr
W www.piperia-seafood.gr

Pisina [81]
25 Akti Themistokleous
Zea Marina
Piraeus, Athens
T 210 451 1324
E ormos@pisina.gr
W www.pisina.gr

Planet Earth [137]
7 Ploutarchou
Kolonaki 10675 Athens
T 210 729 3690
E kkhats@otenet.gr

Workshop:
17 Dorileou
11521 Athens
T/F 210 645 5821

Prosopa [69]
84 Konstantinoupoleos
Gazi, Athens
T 210 341 3433
W www.prosopa.gr

Prytaneion [23]
37 Kolokotroni, Kefalari Square
Kifissia, Athens
T 210 808 9160-2
F 210 808 2577
E info@prytaneion.gr
W www.prytaneion.gr

Rakoselektes [70]
25 Aisopou & Karaiskaki
Psyrri, Athens
T 210 32 22 240

Ratka [33]
30–32 Haritos
Kolonaki 10675 Athens
T 210 729 0746

Rebecca Camhi [62]
80 Themistokleous
Exarchia, Athens
T/F 210 383 7030
E gallery@rebeccacamhi.com
W www.rebeccacamhi.com

Rock 'n' Roll [126]
6 Loukianou & Ypsilantou
Kolonaki, Athens
T 210 721 7127

St George Lycabettus [92]
2 Kleomenous
Kolonaki 10675 Athens
T 210 729 0711
F 210 729 0439
E info@sglycabettus.gr
W www.sglycabettus.gr

Semiramis Hotel [98]
48 Harilaou Trikoupi
Kifissia 14562 Athens
T 210 628 4400
F 210 628 4499
E info@semiramisathens.com
W www.semiramisathens.com

Septem [116]
58 Vasileos Georgiou B
Glyfada 16674 Athens
E escape@balux-septem.com
W www.balux-septem.com

Skipper's Yacht 'n' Roll [76]
Pier 1, Alimos Marina
17455 Athens
T 210 988 0282

**Spathario Museum of
Shadow Theatre** [19]
Vassilissis Sofias & D. Ralli
Kastalias Square
Maroussi 15124 Athens
T 210 612 7245
F 210 612 7206
E info@karagiozismuseum.gr
W www.karagiozis museum.gr

Spondi [113]
5 Pyrronos, Varnava Square
Pangrati 11636 Athens
T 210 752 0658
E spondi@relaischateaux.com
W www.spondi.gr

Ta Kioupia [112]
2 Olympionikon & Dexamenis
Politia Square
Kifissia 14563 Athens
T 210 620 0005
F 210 807 8035
E info@kioupia.com
W www.kioupia.gr

Taverna Xinos [50]
4 Geronta
Plaka, Athens
T 210 322 1065

Technopolis [69]
100 Pireos
Gazi 11854 Athens
T 210 346 1589
W www.cityofathens.gr

Telemachus [23]
19 Fragopoulou
Kifissia, Athens
T 210 807 4015
E gtsili@otenet.gr

Telis [66]
86 Evripidou
Koumoundourou Square
Omonia, Athens
T 210 324 2775

Thanasis [57]
69 Mitropoleos
Monastiraki, Athens
T 210 324 4705

Thes Tziveli [24]
6 Panagitsas
Kifissia, Athens
T 210 623 1217
F 210 623 1218
E tziveli@ath.forthnet.gr
W www.thestziveli.com

Tike [117]
27 Kritis & Harilaou Trikoupi
Kifissia, Athens
T 210 808 4418
F 210 808 4482
E tike@tike.com.tr
W www.tike.com.tr

To Bakaliko Ola Ta Kala [76]
1 Artemidos, Esperidon Square
Glyfada 16675 Athens
T 210 894 4577
F 210 894 3423

To Berdema [20]
20 Leof Vassilissis Amalias
Kifissia, Athens
T 210 801 3853
F 210 623 1134

To Kafenio [33]
26 Loukianou
Kolonaki, Athens
T 210 722 9056

To Kouti [54]
23 Adrianou
Monastiraki 10555 Athens
T 210 321 3229
F 210 321 3029

To Liondari Tou Piraeus [81]
20 Marias Xatzikiriakou
Piraeus 18538 Athens
T 210 451 1118
F 210 451 1152
E info@leonpireas.gr
W www.leonpireas.gr

To Ouzadiko [110]
Lemos Shopping Centre
25–29 Karneadou
Kolonaki, Athens
T 210 729 5484

Trata O Stelios [62]
7 Themistokleous & 9 Nikitara
Omonia 10678 Athens
T 210 383 8531

Twenty One [94]
21 Kolokotroni & Mykonou
Kifissia 14562 Athens
T 210 623 3521
F 210 623 3821
E info@twentyone.gr
W www.twentyone.gr

Tzitzikas & Mermigas [18]
26 Eschylou & Agiou Giorgiou
Halandri, Athens
T 210 681 0529

Varoulko [115]
80 Pireos
Keramicos 10435 Athens
T 210 522 8400
F 210 522 8800
E info@varoulko.gr
W www.varoulko.gr

Varsos Kifissia [19]
5 Kassaveti
Kifissia, Athens
T 210 801 2472
F 210 801 0681
E varsosvl@hol.gr
W www.varsoskifissia.gr

Varvakios Agora [65]
Athinas, between Sofokleous
and Evripidou

Omonia, Athens

Vasso Consola [70]
1–3 Sahtouri & Sari
Psyrri 11553 Athens
T 210 331 9154
F 210 3319669
E vassoconsola@in.gr
W www.vassoconsola.com

**Vouliagmeni Lake &
Health Spa** [79]
Leof Posidonos
Vouliagmeni, Athens
T 210 896 2237
F 210 896 2351

Vrettos [52]
41 Kydathineon
Plaka, Athens
T 210 323 2110

Wild Rose [128]
293 Kifissias
Kifissia, Athens
T 210 801 0810

Yiorgos Eleftheriadis [134]
13 Agion Anargiron
Psyrri 10554 Athens
T/F 210 331 2622
E info@yiorgoseleftheriades.gr
W www.yiorgoseleftheriades.gr

Zen [80]
Vouliagmenis Marina
Vouliagmeni, Athens
T 210 967 0659

SOUNIO, LAVRIO [144]
*For bus information: 210 880 8000.
Buses depart every hour from
Athens Mavromataion, near Pedion
Areos Park (6:30 a.m. to 5:30 p.m).
Travel time to the Temple of
Poseidon is approximately 1 hour
and 30 minutes; across from the
temple is the Cape Sounio Hotel.
The journey to Lavrio takes 1 hour
50 minutes. By car go south
towards Piraeus taking the coastal
Leof Posidonos towards Glyfada.
A shorter, but less scenic route is
to take the Attiki Odos motorway
towards Lavrio.*

AEGINA [150]
POROS [156]
HYDRA [162]
SPETSES [166]
*Tickets to any of the islands are
available from travel agents in
Karaiskaki Square, or quayside at
Piraeus minutes before departure.
Ferries for Aegina depart hourly
from 7:00 a.m. until 8:00 p.m. Other
islands have at least two daily
routes year round, with more
during the high season. Schedule
information can be found at
www.greekferries.gr, or by dialling
the automated voice service (210
414 7800) or the Piraeus Port
Authority (210 459 3000). If travelling
by ferry with your car, it is advisable
to book in advance during the
summer season. Travelling by
hydrofoil to the islands from
Piraeus is quicker, but more
expensive. Travel time to Aegina is
40 minutes, to Poros 1 hour, to
Hydra 90 minutes, and to Spetse
2 hours. Presently all ferries and
hydrofoils for the Saronic islands
leave from gates E7 and E8.*

**NAFPLIO, MYCENAE,
EPIDAUROS** [170]
*For bus information: 210 512 4910/1.
Buses leave every hour from
Kiffisos Station; the journey takes
approximately 2 hours 30 minutes.
Buses also go directly to Mycenae
and Epidauros (2 hours 30
minutes), and from Nafplio to both
sites. To reach Nafpolio by car,
head south towards Corinth,
following the signs for Corinth, and
then Tripoli. After crossing the
Corinth Canal, take the exit for
Nafplio. The Nafplia Palace Resort
is at the opposite end of town,
following the road past the seafront
cafés until you reach the end of the
pier. The hotel is located inside the
Akronafplia fortress; take the lift
inside the mountain to the hotel*

*foyer. To reach Mycenae from
Nafplio, follow the road to Argos
and then turn left into the
archaeological site (approximately
30 minutes). For Epidauros, follow
the signs for Lygourio-Epidauros
(approximately 30 minutes). Local
buses leave from Syngrou Street
(information: 275 202 7493).*

**PARNASSUS,
ARACHOVA** [176]
*For bus information: 210 831 7096.
Buses depart from the Liosion bus
station to Arachova; the journey
takes approximately 2 hours
30 minutes. By car, head north on
the national highway towards
Thessaloniki (Lamia), and take the
exit for Arachova–Delphi (84th km).
Arachova is 8 kilometres from
Delphi; for the Santa Marina Hotel,
follow the signs from the main
street.*

DELPHI, GALAXIDI [182]
*For bus information: 210 831 7096.
Buses depart from the Liosion bus
station to Delphi; the journey takes
approximately 2 hours 30 minutes.
By car, head north on the national
highway for Thessaloniki (Lamia),
and take the exit for Arachova–
Delphi (84th km). Galaxidi is 30
minutes south of Delphi by car, or
can be reached directly from the
local bus station. Osios Lucas
monastery is 24 kilometres towards
Athens.*